DAY TRADING

The Step-by-Step Guide for Beginners.
Money Management, Passive Income, and
Business Psychology. Stock Market
Strategies and Techniques (Forex, Swing,
Options Trading, etc)

Brandon Scott

author is not engaging in the rendering of legal, financial, medical or professional advice. The content within this book has been derived from various sources. Please consult a licensed professional before attempting any techniques outlined in this book. By reading this document, the reader agrees that under no circumstances is the author responsible for any losses, direct or indirect, which are incurred as a result of the use of information contained within this document, including, but not limited to, — errors, omissions, or inaccuracies

TABLE OF CONTENTS

PART ONE
Introduction

Day trading is a hot topic that many people are interested in and wanting to learn more about. This book will give you all the information you need on this to make sure that you are both knowledgeable and successful at the same time. Through this book you will be able to learn how to generate an income with day trading and understand how to manage your profits as well. You will also be able to understand how this works and how to do it successfully while understanding the difference between different types of trading. There are a few different ways that you can trade and understanding this will take the confusion away as many people get confused about this on a regular basis and find themselves making mistakes that can be avoided.

Another issue that people have that we will take care of here as well is the fact that we help you understand where to find the stocks in the first place. Believe it or not, many people don't have the slightest clue on how to find the information on stocks and where to find them which is what we've done here so that you will be able to know it for yourself. In addition to this, we also will be giving you every piece of information you will need on how to make sure that you are scanning in the right manner and that you are able to understand the volume of information that comes with understanding stocks and managing them at the same time. This is going to greatly benefit you with your goals in this field.

We will be teaching you useful skills with this book such as the following items.

- Understanding the right strategies that you need including trading and sizing strategies
- Setting goals for yourself
- Gaining knowledge for yourself
- Avoiding mistakes and problems
- What you need to do to be successful
- Understanding the stock gap
- Having an exit strategy for yourself

We will also delve into the psychology behind this field as well as it's a complex subject that makes more and more people want to understand this field. We speak about this subject because the way your mind is working and the thoughts that your thinking affects how you interact with other people and how you will approach this field as well.

There are certain beliefs about this field that are right and wrong and one of the things that we will be doing for you is making sure that you are able to see what is an actual truth and what is something that people misconstrue and think is an actual thing but is not.

When you become involved in this field there is a plethora of things that you will need to know and this book is dedicated to making sure that you have as much information as possible so that you have the highest chance of success possible and so you will be able to do this like a professional with minimal risks.

Chapter 1: What Is Day Trading?

In day trading, you get to buy and sell the underlying asset or instrument on the same day, in a way that all the positions are closed by the time the market closes in the trading day. Most of the traders that engage in day trading are speculators. The main aim at the end of each trade is to get to walk away with profits that you are happy about. Day trading is more of a short-term investment. At the end of the day, you either walk away with a profit or a loss. It also provides a chance to take part in multiple trades. As a beginner, this may not be a good start-up strategy. You cannot be engaging in more than two trades when you do not have adequate information on how you can go about different trades. Making rushed decisions to get in trades without proper planning is like setting yourself up for failure. You know that you are going to fail, yet you proceed with the plan. Be careful to free yourself from such occurrences in life. If you are a beginner, you can start by understanding how the whole process works before committing yourself to engage in the trade.

To avoid negative price gaps resulting in the difference between the day's closing price and the next day's opening price, day traders get to exit positions before the market closes. This exit also protects them from unmanageable risks that they may not be able to tackle. Day traders utilize margin leverage while carrying out different trades. For most brokers, the acceptable leverage margin is 4:1, which can be reduced to 2:1 by the end of the day. The popular financial instruments that traders engage in include currencies, options, stocks, host of future contracts, and contracts for difference. Depending on the instrument that you find suitable, you can carry out the trade that you wish to be part of. As you decide to trade, you will require a broker, through which you can use to carry out your different trades. As you select the best broker, there are some factors that you will have to consider. As you keep reading, you will come across these factors that will guide you in getting the best broker.

Day trading is a profitable investment, and there is a lot that you can make as a trader. The different trading strategies and trading plan will help you stay on top of your game as a trader. In the book, I have tried to provide information that will help you become a better trader. I will not promise that it will be an easy journey. The steps that you take toward becoming a better trader will set you apart despite the bumps that you will come across. Anybody can make a good trader as long as they have the right attitude.

Chapter 2: Why Trade Options?

Generate an Income

As an investor, you are looking for a venture that will generate capital for you. This goal makes you focus on opportunities that bring profits, and it helps you avoid all the factors that can expose the venture to risks that result in a loss. We have individuals who are making a fortune out of day trading. As a beginner, one of the focuses that you have is to become a master of the game. In any business, we have people that are making it and those that are struggling and barely making ends meet. The different approaches to what we are doing bring a difference in our output. Depending on how good your approach is, you can equally earn an amount that measures up to the work that you give. It is without any doubt that there are different levels for different traders in the industry. Some are at the peak of their careers where they are earning a lot. At the same time, there are some people who are struggling with average results and barely making it. After engaging in trade, they all walk out with different incomes. The climax of a trader is getting to a point where they easily make successful trades and earn a fortune from them. Getting to this point is possible as long as you are committed to putting in the work.

Is there a limit amount in day trading? Well, people ask this to know what to expect when they get on top and become experts. I do not think that there is a limited amount that you can earn while trading options. The only limit you can have is the one that you have set individually if you decide that you only need half a million from the trades you make per month that is likely the figure that you will get at the end. At the same time, you can set some big figures that you expect to match up to, so you put in a lot of effort into ensuring that you get to the point that you aspire to get to. You ensure that you are fully devoted to hitting the target; this will see you place a lot of effort and hard work in ensuring that you get the results that you desire. At the end of the day, we are who we choose to become. If you choose to have a limited mentality, you get average results. Alternatively, if you decide that you are not a limited edition, you stretch to further horizons and get to exceed your expectations. I choose to believe that the income one generates from day trading is not limited to certain figures. You get to decide what you are worth and chose to define who you are by making the best decisions regarding what you are doing.

Profits With Low Investment

With day trading, the profits that you collect are not limited to the investment that you make. The idea that you can only make huge profits with a big investment happens to be a myth. A good trader is not defined by how big their investment is, but rather by how well they play their cards. You find that even while gambling, the individual with more to lose does not always stand the upper chance at winning. As a gambler, you might be having very little to offer and still win the gamble. The differentiating factor at the end of the day is the strategy that you use to win the gamble. With a very good plan, you can walk away as the winner, even if you had little to offer. This also happens in life. You find that the individual who managed to take a good win home had little, yet a proper and well-structured plan got them to acquire the win among the people who had more. The plan and approach used are essential to success. It helps you find the best angle to attack the situation at hand and makes you successful at it. The idea that you need to have more to get more will not always work. With little, you can decide to turn over the situation to a more favorable outcome. The idea is not limited to the amount of revenues that you have to bring to the table; the problem should be how far you are willing to go to get what you want.

Can our expectations make us want to invest in more? Most defiantly, yes. With an ambition of wanting to become an overnight success, you might find yourself making decisions that do not go well for you. At that point, you have very big expectations of becoming a millionaire. There is a certain definition you have for success that is according to what you like and what you believe in. You find that you are willing to break your neck just to get to the point that you aspire. At times, these desires can be harmful, especially when you have very high expectations. You are likely to make wrong decisions and not take your time carefully planning your ways. To avoid finding yourself in such situations, it is important that you learn to have a realistic approach to your goals. In this case, you get to retain the goals that you have in mind as you come up with a realistic approach to tackle different trades. As you begin, it would be best if you started out with a small investment. Even as you start out with small profits, you can start earning bigger profits in the future. The plan is first to get ahold of the activities that surround a trade. Identify the different factors influencing the trade as you come up with ways to make successful trades. In the end, you learn how to convert your knowledge into a sustainable income.

Insurance

We are currently in space and time, where people appreciate the need for insurance. It is always good to secure your investments from the possible risks that may arise. Different insurance companies have different insurance plans. They want to ensure that they offer services that their clients can easily relate to and buy. The benefits of having insurance are many. One of the key benefits of insurance is that it protects one from the possibility of incurring a complete loss. Supposing you purchased a gadget today, and it got broken the next day. You would have incurred a complete loss if you had not taken insurance. With insurance, you can easily get compensated for the loss. This can be done by being given another similar but used gadget or getting a new gadget. At the end of the day, you do not incur a complete loss. Life is unpredictable. One day, you are healthy, and the next day, you are involved in a bad accident that leaves you fighting for your life. Such an event is not planned, so there may come a time when you are unable to cater to the accumulated bills. In such a situation, your challenge can be well-tackled if you have medical insurance, for instance. It allows you to take care of your bills, and you are easily treated without having to break your back to cater to the bills.

The other benefit of having insurance is that you do not get to start over after a misfortune. In a situation where you had a big business that encountered misfortune in the form of a fire or any accident that can sabotage the business, you can easily use your insurance cover the expenses and get out of the mess. As a businessman, you must not encounter a complete loss. The insurance helps you to pick up from the loss incurred and turn it into a successful outcome. Some losses can be difficult to recover from. Once they happen, it could mean that it is the end of a successful venture. At that point, you not only encounter a loss in terms of capital, but it also translates to an unachieved dream. To ensure that you do not get to this point in life, the insurance companies help you in avoiding complete losses. You might be wondering how you get insurance as a trader. Well, your trading portfolio acts as insurance. You can be assured of safe and secure transactions if you have a good trading portfolio. The portfolio is an indication of your trading success or failure. Each trader aims to create a good portfolio as it can open up other opportunities for you in the future. The trading industry experiences different seasons. There are times when it will experience a loss and, at other times, a profit. In case of a loss, the trader can use their portfolio as insurance. It can help them minimize the probability of incurring a complete loss.

Limited Loss of Profit

The worst thing that can happen in your investment is for it to incur a loss. Each investor dreads the idea of having to incur a loss. You want to ensure that you maximize the profits as you minimize the potential of making losses. One of the best ways to ensure that you keep earning is making sure that you have a proper risk management plan. It is close to impossible to run a risk-free venture. Among the external and internal factors surrounding a venture, there are some risks that are involved. The plan is to succeed in coming up with ways where you can counter the risks and end up with a profitable business. Day trading has its own risks that expose it to the possibility of resulting in a loss. However, the plan and approach that you have can help you in avoiding the risks and maximizing your profits. The main differentiating factor among the individuals who are making it today and those who are failing is the plan that they have to achieve what they want. I have come across some people who are afraid of engaging in a trade due to fear of incurring a loss. You find that they have some misguided beliefs that since another person failed, they will also fail. Well, someone's fate may not be your own. Hence, just because they experienced various challenges that made them not succeed in the industry, it does not mean that you will encounter the same fate. We are all different, and we choose to define our own paths.

With the right attitude to learn, it will be easy to make it in the trading industry. One of the best investments that you can make is dedicating your time and money in learning the skills required. Most people start trading with very little knowledge and skills on how to go about it, and they end up taking a loss in their investment. If you are looking forward to earning from the investment that you make, it is equally investing more in making the investment a success. The biggest game-changer in getting the best results is determined by the kind of attitude that you have. The willingness to learn will open doors for you and help you achieve more than you expected. As an investor, learning is a process that you have to be well aware of the industry where you are in and appreciate it for you to get far. Being aware of the different strategies that you can utilize, depending on the situation at hand, will help you in avoiding the losses that you are likely to come across. It goes without saying that you will need to be committed to what you are doing for you to produce the best results. At times, the results may not be as fast as you would have expected. There are times when you will have to exercise patience and trust in the process. When you master the art of trading and are well acquitted with the best tactics to use, it becomes easy to minimize the losses.

PART TWO
HOW IT WORKS
Chapter 3: How Day Trading Works

Like any other investment that you can take part in, day trading is designed to earn you a profit at the end of the day. You can turn it into a successful career that you can use to sustain your livelihood. There are some heated debates among different individuals, with concerns if you can generate a sustainable income from trading. Well, I would say that it is possible since we already have individuals that are literally living from it. I think how we choose to trade has a major impact on the results that we get at the end of the trade. One of the biggest factors contributing to trading success is having the right information. Take time to get the information right from the beginning. You might have started your trading career recently. But your willingness to learn sets you apart from the rest. Like any journey, the goal is to get to the destination. Your mode of transport may vary, and it will bring a difference in the time you will arrive and the comfort that you will get. The same applies to day trading. Some people easily earn from it, and at the same time, there are those who have many regrets that they engaged in the trade in the first place. Choose the path that you wish to take as you start your trading career. The years of experience may not matter, but the determination that you have to learn more will get you far.

The strategies that you decide to settle for will determine the outcome of the majority of the trades that you make. As a good trader, you need to have a good trading plan that will help you while trading. In this book, you will come across some tips that will make your trading career worth your while. You need to be open to the challenges that you will encounter as a trader. There are some risks that will expose your trade to the potential of suffering a loss, and you need to be open to the whole idea. At the same time, you need to be familiar with the different risk management plans that you can engage in to ensure that you have an easy time managing the risks that you come across. Trading is not an easy venture that you get to joy-ride in and still walk away with profits. The efforts that you make in getting better at trading will set you apart and ensure that you become a better trader. There are some moments that you will feel proud of the decisions that you made, and other times, you will wish that you never made those decisions. You have to be okay with the idea that you may get a loss or a profit. In the book, I have outlined some of the tips that you can use to ensure your trading success. With the right plan and strategy, you will make a living out of day trading.

Chapter 4: Day Trading vs. Swing Trading

In day trading, the traders engage in a market with fast-moving commodities (underlying assets), while in swing trading, the traders purchase stocks that are not perishable and get to hold them for a while until they generate a profit. This is when they trade them. We shall discuss the differences and similarities between day trading and swing trading

Similarities Between Day Trading and Swing Trading

1. *High profits*

   Both swing trading and day trading have the potential of earning you a huge profit. The amount that you get to take home at the end of the day depends on the effort that you are willing to put and how well you plan your trades. You find that in a given industry, there are people who are doing more than others. The main difference between those who are making it and who are struggling lies in the efforts that they are willing to make. They say that there is no traffic when you go the extra mile. Doing more than what others are doing will set you apart and get you places. If you are a trader taking part in swing or day trading, you can stay assured that you can equally earn big from your investment.

2. *Trading platforms*

There are some trading platforms that can be used by both swing and day traders. At times, you may not be sure what exactly you want to do. In such moments, you want to engage in a platform that offers a variety of opportunities. If you find that you are better placed in day trading, you can decide to engage in it fully, and at the same time, if you find swing trading to be the better solution for you, you can easily go with it. Such a trading platform offers convenience. You do not have to go through the hassles of getting another broker all over again. You can switch to a trade that you are comfortable with and still remain on the same platform. You might also decide to invest in both trading options. After doing your survey and you want to engage in more than one investment, you can do both swing and day trading from the same platform.

3. *Unlimited number of stocks*

In both swing trading and day trading, there is no limit on the number of stocks that you can engage in. When it comes to day trading, you can engage in multiple trades in a day, and the same applies to swing trading. As you do this, be careful to stick to the maximum dollar rule. You do so to ensure that you minimize the potential of getting huge losses that you may not be able to recover from. As you trade in an unlimited number of stocks, ensure that you make the right trading decisions.

Differences Between Day Trading and Swing Trading

1. *Investment plan*

   Day trading is more of a short term investment, while swing trading is more of a long term investment. In day trading, you can get a chance to carry out various trades during the day. By the end of the day, you get your returns, and you can know if you made a profit or a loss. On a good day, and with proper trading strategies, you can easily walk away with a huge profit that you will celebrate. You can still experience a bad day where most trades become unsuccessful and end up with a lot of frustration. With swing trading, you get to purchase stocks and keep them to trade at a later day. You can hold the stocks for days, weeks, or even a month. At this time, you will be waiting for the stock to grow into a bigger potential profit. When it does, you can easily trade.

2. *Risks*

When it comes to the level of exposure to high risks, day trading takes the trophy home. There are plenty of risks in which day trading is exposed to. As you get a chance to conduct multiple trades, the trades are exposed to different varieties of risks. You find that the risk management that worked for a given trade may not work for the other trades that you make. This creates the need to keep learning new strategies to counter the different risks that the trade is exposed to. On the other hand, swing trading is not challenged with many risks. You get to buy the stock as you wait for the best time to engage in a trade. The long duration gives you the chance to evaluate all risks involved and helps you avoid the chance of encountering more risks.

3. *Time*

As a day trader, you find that you need to spend much of your time looking into different trades and coming up with the best strategies to use to succeed. Most of the individuals who engage in day trading are usually full-time traders. The need to put more focus on trade makes them spend much of their time figuring out how best they can trade. Swing traders are the part-time traders since the trade does not require much of their effort and time. They can easily handle other businesses even as they trade.

4. *Decision making*

Individuals who are quick in making decisions stand a better chance at succeeding in day trading. You find that they make a lot of trading decisions in a day, and they have to ensure that the decisions made are the best, so they do not incur a loss. With swing trading, you get more time to decide on the trades that you want to make and how you want to make them. For individuals who take time to decide, this can be the best trading option that they can work with. It allows time to evaluate decisions before coming to a conclusion properly.

Chapter 5: Buying Long, Selling Short Retail, and Institutional High-Frequency Trading (HFT)

Buying Long

A long trade commences from buying a stock with the plan of selling at a higher price in the future. Depending on the trading software that you are using, you will have an entry button marked long or buy. Both terms are used interchangeably to mean the same thing while trading. You will come across some traders saying that they are going long; this means that they are willing to buy some underlying stocks or any financial instrument that they would like to take part in. For instance, I could be showing some interest in buying shares from the apple company. You might find me saying that I want to go long on 100 shares of Apple stock. In this investment plan, there is a high likelihood of acquiring huge profits.

The price of the underlying asset is expected to rise with time. If you bought the shares at $100 each, you might be selling them at $120 at a later date.

Selling Short Retail

When it comes to short trades, the trader can sell the underlying asset before purchasing them; at this time, they hope that the prices will lower so they can earn a profit. As a new trader, you may be confused by this trade and fail to understand how it works. Primarily, we are used to the idea of purchasing something. Then we get to sell it. It might be a challenge if you are now introduced to a concept where you sell items that you do not have. In the trading market, you can either buy the financial instruments or sell them, or you can sell then you buy. The decisions that you make are based on what you feel comfortable with as a trader. At times, you will come across traders using the term short and sell interchangeably. For instance, I could say that I will short my shares in a given company. When I say so, I mean that I want to sell the shares that I have in the said company. If you are a professional trader, you can easily earn a profit from short trades.

Institutional Traders High-Frequency Trading (HFT)

HFT is a big automated trading platform that is utilized by institutional investors, hedge funds, and investment banks. It uses very powerful computers to carry out huge transactions of orders at a very high speed. In this trading platform, it is possible to carry out multiple trades. At the same time, it is possible to scan the market in small duration, and thus, it gives the institutional traders an added advantage in the open market. The system uses a complex algorithm while performing various functions. Traders using HFT are more advantaged than those utilizing other methods.

Chapter 6: How to Find Stocks for Trade

On any given day, there are thousands and thousands of stocks that you can trade on. To the untrained eye, the potential number of trade opportunities can really feel overwhelming. Also, picking popular stocks like Google or Apple, or simply playing IPOs and hoping for a quick flip based on their hype, is a strategy that you need to do away with, as much as it may work.

To be perfectly frank, finding the best stocks to trade with will require a lot of work and plenty of research on your part. So if you are hoping to simply find a list of high-volume stocks to trade with every day and make lots and lots of money, you might as well end your reading here.

With so many choices of stock out there, it can be quite an overwhelming task to identify the right stocks to include in your watchlist. So, how do you identify what stocks are best suited to day trading? In this chapter, I will elaborate on some of the basic tips you can use to identify the best stocks to trade with. Read on to find out.

But first, let us get familiar with stock gaps.

Stock Gap

During the after-hours of trading, stock shares will often move up or down in value. As a consequence, stocks will open at a different price compared to the price when it closed the previous trading day. A **Gap Up** is when a stock opens higher than the previous closing price, and a **Gap Down** is when a stock opens lower than the previous closing price.

Primarily, news catalysts are the reason that stock values will move lower or higher than their previous day's closing price. Analyst upgrades and downgrades, quarterly earnings releases, and press releases are some of the factors that could bring about the stock gaps.

Finding the Right Gappers to Trade

There are hundreds of stocks gapping up and down with every passing day. The best ones to trade, however, will depend on your trading style, and what your strategy is. That considered, the most explosive stocks for day trading generally have the following characteristics.

- ✓ A large intraday range
- ✓ A high relative volume
- ✓ Low-float
- ✓ News catalysts
- ✓ No resistance for a long play
- ✓ No support for a short play

So, with thousands of stocks gapping up and down daily, how do you decide on which ones to trade with on that day and which ones you should leave alone? Here is where a **Stock Scanner** comes in.

A stock scanner is a useful tool for filtering out the best momentum stocks from the subpar ones. It can quickly and easily narrow down your options to the best 20 stocks gapping each day, and it uses gap percentage, volume, and float—the most important factors that determine the ability of a stock to make big moves on that day.

Day traders usually lay their focus on high-volume stocks that are having significant price movements because these are the stocks that offer the best opportunities for making them some quick money. Stocks with a high relative volume, low float, ones that are gapping below support, and the ones that are gapping above the resistance all have a pretty high interest.

Furthermore, there exist scanners called **Bounce Scanners,** which are used basically to show you the stocks that are extended to the downside but are due for a bounce back. Also, there are **Pull-Back Scanners** for stocks that are extended to the upside but are bound to run out of momentum.

When to Run the Stock Scans

1. Night Scans

Each day before the market opens, you should run scans so as to get a picture of what stocks moved during that trading day. In addition, you might want to run scans after the closure of the post-market trading, usually at 8 pm. This scan lets you see all the big movers from that trading day, and you also get to see which stocks are making moves after hours in reaction to news events. This way, you can make your watchlist for the upcoming trading day.

2. Morning Scans

A lot of companies do their press releases at around 8 to 8:30 in the morning, and we know stock values react swiftly to these releases. You might want to run morning scans since these show you which stocks are moving pre-market, so you will be able to know all the best stocks that could be in play during that trading day. So when the bell rings and the trading begins, you will know just what to do to make you some money.

How to Choose Stocks for Day Trading

Day trading is a high-risk investment strategy that requires a lot of knowledge, diligence, patience, expertise, and, most importantly, a plan. The stocks you trade with will depend on a number of factors. The amount of capital you have available, your level of experience, and your trading strategy are just but some of the factors in play.

So, before you decide to start day trading, you'll need to figure out what stocks are on your radar and focus on them. More importantly, you should write down your criteria for picking stocks as part of your trading plan. This trading plan is dynamic, and, as such, it will evolve as you go on learning and uncovering your weaknesses and strengths.

Before you pick stocks, here are a few things to consider.

- ✓ Understand the level of risk involved, and decide whether it is appropriate to you or not.
- ✓ Know yourself, and develop a smart strategy for identifying and choosing the stocks to invest in

✓ Keep it simple. Start by focusing on and analyzing just one stock.

✓ Learn to use trading charts to understand stock movements and the overall market.

✓ Stick to your plan!

So how do you choose stocks for trading?

1. *Consider YOUR position*

   The stocks you end up choosing for your day trading strategy, like everything else in your financial matters, should be tailored to your personal situation and the goals that you aim to achieve. After all, this is not a one-size-fits-all type of situation. Take into consideration the amount of capital you have available, and the type of investing that you are going to indulge in. Consider the sectors that best resonate with your personality, values, and your personal needs.

   For instance, if you are 60 years old, then you would certainly want to think things through before making a definitive decision, and you want to make just a little extra money to spend each month. As such, you are maybe trading with low volatility stocks that might be more appropriate to you. On the other hand, if you are a 24-year-old with a fast mind and in need of plenty of action to stay focused, then short-term and volatile stocks may be right for you.

Either way, whatever decision you make, think it through. Understand that stocks have different levels of volatility and the velocity of price movements. Be sure to do your research by reading up on company financials and studying the market trends. That way, you have an idea of which stocks are the hare and which are the tortoise.

2. *Keep risk management at the back of your palm*
   As I had stated earlier, day trading is a high-risk investment strategy. So before you get started on anything, determine your tolerance for risk. Have an idea of the degree of risk you can afford and live

with. Direct your focus on creating a stock selecting strategy that is designed to control risk and preserve your capital since this should be your most important objective.

In the market, there is a wide spectrum of stock to trade with, each with varying levels of price, volume, and volatility characteristics. You should start out by minimizing the risk. As your experience, skills, finesse, and rate of success increase, you can go on to expand on the risk associated with the stocks you choose to trade with.

So, if your day trading strategy is to "just start trading" or "see how it goes," you need to flush that one out of your system with immediate effect. Instead of having this mindset, analyze, calculate, and make some educated trading decisions.

3. *After you have chosen the stocks to invest in. Keep it simple!!*

Whatever the stock selection strategy you opt to use over the short term or long term, the best thing to do is by keeping it simple. Begin by trading with just one stock. Watch its performance, study it, and learn it. Every stock has its own characteristics and personality, so you need to understand their tendencies to be able to anticipate the right moves

Study its charts at numerous time frames— intraday, daily, and weekly. Learn it. Breathe it. Over time, go ahead and add one more stock and then another, and so on. Now, as you are trading with the one stock you have fully grasped, you can go ahead and learn the behavior of a few other stocks and learn their tendencies.

After you have progressed further along the learning curve, you can now start trading with the stock that you have been studying. Since you have been watching them closely, you already have an understanding of their behaviors. Above all, lay your focus on the stocks that align with your trading strategy and ones that are consistent.

4. *Find the best stocks to day trade with pre-market movers*

The pre-market is the street's favorite way to kick off the day. Those who have been day trading for a while now will bear witness to this. This is because, for one, you get the 'early bird catches the worm' advantage. Horning in on the stocks that are making gains in the pre-market essentially gets your fingers on the pulse of what is going on in the market on that day.

By taking your time to focus and scan these pre-market movers in the early hours, you get the chance to do your research and identify the catalysts before another trader tune in. That way, you make yourself a detailed trading plan ready to go such that when the market opens, you already know where the action is, and you are set to get the ground running.

So, if you want to kick-start your day of trading after a generous lie in, do not be surprised when you find yourself struggling to make a profit. Irrespective of which approach best suits your trading style, the one thing that is needed for each selection process is that you must get an early start to the trading day. The market is getting faster due to an increase in trading volumes. What am trying to say is that by 8 am, you need to be up and get ready for the day ahead

Rules of Stocks Selection

1. Rule 1: Liquidity, Liquidity, and More Liquidity

In the financial world, liquidity basically refers to how quickly an asset can be sold or bought in the market. Therefore, liquid stocks tend to be more discounted, easily traded, and cheaper than other stocks. These stocks usually have significant volumes, where large quantities can be acquired and sold without majorly affecting the prices.

Since most intraday trading plans rely on precise timing and speed, the huge volumes make getting in and out of trades quite easy. Additionally, the equities offered by corporations with higher market caps are usually more liquid compared to those offered by corporations with lower market capitalizations. This is due to the fact that it is easier to find sellers and buyers for that particular asset in question.

2. Rule 2: Volatility of The Stock in Question

A stock is considered volatile if the corporation issuing it experiences variances in their cash flows. That said, stocks that display more volatility tend to do well with most day-trading strategies, and those with low volatility should make you wary about trading with them.

For any day trader, uncertainty in the market makes a mouth-watering trading environment. This is because they actually require movement of prices in order to make money, so they mostly focus on high-volume stocks that have significant price movements.

For the most part, markets will anticipate these changes and react accordingly, but when extenuating circumstances occur, day traders can capitalize on the asset mispricing. For example, if a certain stock opens down 12 % and stays there, then it is not going to have some trading action. But if the stock opens down at 12 %, and after a while, you notice that it is down by 13 % or 14 % or it is back up by 7 % or 8 %, that particular stock is moving, and it may be worth taking a look at for a trade.

3. *Rule 3: Check out the Volumes*

Volume is simply concerned with the total or an overall number of shares or stocks traded in a market for a specific period, and each transaction adds up to the total volume. It acts as an indicator giving weights to market moves. If there is a sudden increase, the strength of that move is reliant on the volume during that time period. Essentially, the bigger the volume, the significant the move.

If you have a substantial amount of capital backing you, you might want to check out stocks with significant volumes. Sure, your brokerage account will give you a list of the top 20 stocks, but the best thing you can do is widen your search a little more. That way, you will be poised to find opportunities that are not on the radars of other traders.

Search for stocks that have a spike in their volumes. For instance, if a stock normally trades 1.2 million shares each day, but then you notice that it has traded 5 million shares by 11 am, that could be an avenue worth exploring.

Your Entry and Exit Strategy

You may have succeeded in selecting the sweetest stock in the globe, but actually profiting from it will depend on strategies. Intraday trading strategies are as many as traders themselves, but by adhering to certain guidelines and looking out for certain day trading signals, you are better positioned to succeed.

Here are some of the guidelines.

1. *Don't get emotionally attached to any particular stock*

   Keep in mind that day trading is all about finding patterns that help you decide when and where you can enter and exit and make a profit or minimize your losses. The stock that makes you money today may not do the same tomorrow. Also, be up to date with the news and current happenings of the financial world. This doesn't necessarily mean you have to be attached to your TV screen. Rather, know what the economic calendar looks like and when your earning season is. That way, you will be able to identify potential stocks for your trading day.

2. *Trade with the current intraday trends*

   The best description of the market movement is 'moving in waves.' As a trader, your job is to ride the waves and nothing else. During an uptrend, you are better off taking long positions. On the other hand, during a downtrend, you might want to take short positions. These intraday trends, however, do not go on indefinitely. One or two trade can be squeezed in before a reversal occurs. When a dominant trend shifts, begin trading with the new trend.

3. *Trade strong stocks in an uptrend and weak ones in a downtrend ·*

When the market prices are moving higher, day traders should look to acquire stocks that are aggressively moving up more than their futures. When the futures actually pull back, a strong stock may not pull back at all, or it will pull back but not as much. These are the stocks that lead the market higher, and they should be traded in an uptrend since they have more potential for profit.

When the indexes are dropping, it is profitable to sell stocks that drop more than the market. This is because when the futures move high in the downtrend, weak stocks will not move up as much, and they may not even move at all. These stocks have a greater potential for profit as the market is falling.

4. *Take your profits regularly*

Day traders usually have very little time to capture their profits, and as such, they must spend as little time as possible in trades that are losing them money or trending in the wrong direction. Here are two simple ways that you can use to capture your profits when you are day trading with the trends.

- In an uptrend, capture your profits at, or slightly above, the prior high price in the current trend.
- In a downtrend, take your profits at, or slightly below, the prior low price in the current trend

5. *When the market stalls, hold your hand*

There are times when the market will not trend. Sometimes, the intraday trends change so frequently that it becomes hard to establish an overriding direction. If the major highs and lows cannot be made out, then make sure that the intraday moves are big enough for the potential reward for exceeding the risk.

If the price is not trending, you are better off switching to a range-bound trading strategy, during which the drawn lines are horizontal and not angled. The same general concepts apply. When buying, you should focus on exiting near the top of the range, but not at the very top. When selling, you should look to exit in the lower section of the range, but not at the very bottom.

Remember that day trading is a risky endeavor, one that requires a lot of knowledge, skill, and self-control, and plenty of patience. If you are looking to make a big win by staking your money on your gut feelings, you should try the casino.

Chapter 7: Tools and Platforms That Brokers Use

How to Select a Good Brokerage Account

1. *Reviews provided by account users*

   There is a lot that you can pick from the different reviews provided by users. The account users can openly express themselves by giving feedback for how they felt while using the product being discussed. It's more of a safe space to give an open opinion. On the other hand, it is highly likely that people give a false opinion. Considering that this is a place that they have invested in, they talk from a personal point of view. As a trader, at the beginning of your trading career, you want to ensure that you make the right decisions in all the steps that you are going to undertake. Any single mistake done will automatically sabotage your entire trading career. Selecting the best brokerage accounts will be one of the best decisions that you make. It will ensure that you have a smooth trading experience without much hassle. Some of the reviews can be accessed online on different sites. At the same time, if the broker has a social media page, you can go through it and find out what people have to say regarding the broker and the services provided. In case you come across some red flags, they should automatically make you avoid engaging the broker. On the other hand, good reviews show you that you can go ahead to use the brokerage account.

2. *Research*

Doing proper research will save you the pain of getting frustrated. Many times, we jump into conclusions without solid evidence and end up getting harmed in the process. The whole point of researching is accessing solid evidence that can back up your decision. In a fast-growing industry, it is highly expected that you come across cons. These are people who want to take advantage of others by stealing from them. Currently, there are many brokers, and not all have your best interest at hand. Some come up with an attractive and tempting plan that lures traders into opening accounts with them. In the end, they end up scamming many people and going with their hard-earned money. To avoid becoming a victim of such fraudsters purporting to be brokers, make sure that you do your research well. You can easily get this information from different websites, journals, blogs, and social media platforms and from reading different books. Considering that you are looking for a platform to invest your money, you cannot afford to sleep at your job. You need a platform that secures your investment and ensures that you earn an income that can sustain your lifestyle. If you are a beginner, the first initial stages should be spent doing thorough research to ensure that you make the best decisions at the end of it all. Do not rush getting a brokerage account without proper research on the account.

3. Investment style

Different brokerage accounts offer different investment strategies. After doing your research, you will find the investment strategy that you would like to engage in. If you want a buy-and-hold investment plan, where you get to buy shares and hold them until they mature and become profitable, you can get a good broker that supports that. In this case, you are looking for a broker who can best ensure that you have a good time investing in day trading. When it comes to day trading, you will be conducting trades and getting results on the same day. With each day, you conduct your trades, and in the end, you find out if it was a success or if you incurred a loss. For a day trader, you will be engaging in short-term investment. The broker that you decide to settle with should offer a favorable plan for such an investor. They need to ensure that all your needs are properly handled so that you can get the best outcome while investing. As a trader, you also need to identify if you are a passive or an active investor. As a day trader, you are more likely an active investor. You want an account that facilitates all the features to ensure that you have an exemplary trading experience, which will have an impact on the results that you get from the trades that you make on a daily basis.

4. *The cost*

At the end of the day, you want to get an account that is within your budget. You want to ensure that you do not stretch beyond your limits to the point that will leave you broke at the end of the investment. As a beginner, you want to be careful with the amount of money that you are willing to spend. We have had some individuals spending beyond what they can afford to lose. One thing with investments is that they can either turn out to be successful or at the same time, result in being a complete loss. Since all this is a possibility and you cannot be really certain that you will end up with a profit, it is best if you avoid making a major risk. The more you advance, the more you can be open to taking bigger risks. At that point, you will have more from the different investments that you make, so in case of anything, it becomes easy to manage the situation. Interestingly, this is a topic that most seem to have different opinions and concerns. Some say that the more you give out, the more you get. Others say that it is what you do with the investment that gets you to the point where you aspire to get to, so in this case, you can decide to start small and have the right strategy and plan that can get you great returns. Either way, you can evaluate and gauge what you can handle and decide to go with what suits you best.

Factors to Consider in a Brokerage Account

1. *Customer services provided*

   It goes without saying that it is the desire of every client to get the best services from that service provider. You want reliable, convenient, and trustworthy service providers who do not compromise in terms of the quality that they offer.

The best broker is one that offers the best customer service experience to the users. On matters regarding the service provided, you can easily get information from the reviews that the clients give. You will be better placed if you get a broker whom you can easily contact. This means that in case you have any questions regarding your account, you can easily contact them through emails, calls, or any other mode of communication. At the same time, you need a broker who fully supports your trading experience. You find that there are some brokers who provide extra services to their users. For instance, they can provide some analysis of the different trades. From the graphs and charts provided, you can learn a lot about the trade. This makes your trading experience easy, and you can easily make wise decisions while trading. We can use a real-life example to see the impact of good services. If you get in a restaurant and you are immediately attended to, and everything is done really well, you are likely to go back to the same restaurant another time. At the same time, if things are not done as you would have expected, you are less likely to go back to the same restaurant. The same applies to the brokers; you select them based on the services that they provide.

2. *Security*

As you make an investment, you want to ensure that your investment is secure. This means that all the information that you share with the investment is in safe hands and, at the same time, ensures that your money is well protected. In a brokerage account, you will be expected to fill in some personal information, such as bank details and other money transfer details. The investment will involve the exchange of currency, depending on the currency used by the broker. You might be exchanging cash or virtual currency, such as bitcoins. In all the transfers, you want a company that guards your information and ensure that it is not used in a way that is harmful. On the other hand, you want a company that keeps your money safe. You will be making an investment, and your goal is to leap from what you have sowed. Having a company that ensures your money is guarded well will help facilitate a smooth trading experience. With the high rise in brokers, there are some who have bad intentions of conning investors. You have to be keen not to come across such people, so you do not end up making a loss at the end of the day. It is the goal of all investors to get a broker who secures their investment.

3. *Market access*

The market access that you are looking for as a trader depends on how far you see yourself getting in the trading industry. You might be limited to the local market, or you might be the ambitious type that looks forward to the international market. Depending on the vision that you have for your trading career, you can make a wise decision that best suits your plan and dream. Different brokers have different market access. Some people are focused on a small-scale venture. Such mainly deal with the local market. There are some who are focused on a large-scale venture. Such brokers tend to have a wider vision and support an international market. When you decide to trade, you need to know the direction that you want to take in the trading industry. With wider market access, it broadens your opportunities, and you have a variety of trades to choose from. I do not want to sound biased, and we still have people earning a lot from engaging in a local market. It all narrows down to how you are able to strike deals and get the best results from the choices that you make. In the book, you will realize that I majorly focus on the importance of gaining knowledge and having the right information. With the right trading plan and approach, you can make a fortune from any type of market access.

4. *Rates and commissions*

The rates and commissions vary, depending on the broker that you use. For a favorable trading experience, you need a broker with good rates and commissions. From the profits that you get from the different trades that you make, the trader goes home with some percentage of the profit. You need a broker who does not chop off a huge percentage of your income. You need to keep earning for the investment to keep working. This means that the amount that you correct after every trade is of great importance. Getting a broker who takes almost all your earnings means that you will end your venture long before you earn much from it. As you select the best broker to engage, look for one who offers favorable rates that you can work with. You want a rate that ensures you remain in business, and at the same time, you want to encounter growth. Some of the information on the rates is easily accessible from different platforms. However, as you focus on rates, make sure that they are not your main focus. There are some individuals who have incurred major losses from engaging with brokers who offer low rates. You find that some of them use it as a strategy to lure more clients. Once they get them, they end up stealing from them. At times, cheap is expensive. The idea is not going for the cheapest; the idea is going for a good broker with favorable rates that you can work with.

PART THREE

DAY TRADING STRATEGIES

Chapter 8: Day Trading, Trade Management, and Position Sizing Strategies

Important Day Trading Strategies

1. *Knowledge*

One of the defense mechanisms that you can adapt to make it in any industry is having the right knowledge to tackle what you are doing. Most traders engaging in the industry are half-baked. You get little knowledge regarding day trading, and you decide to trade with the little information that you have. At the end of the day, you end up making a loss, which makes you regret the choices that you have made. Making such unwise decisions has seen most people fail to succeed in the industry, and, in turn, they have concluded that day trading is a scam. Ideally, you cannot master something that you are not well aware of. In this case, you cannot become an expert trader with little knowledge of trading. Aside from trading, this applies to all other aspects of life. You find that for us to succeed in anything, we have to be well prepared for the task that is ahead of us. On a daily basis, we have different competitions being held across the world. The contestants have to come up with strategies that give them an added advantage over their competitors. One of the strategies that they will incorporate will involve being well conversant with all the details regarding the task they will be performing. The one who knows more is better placed than the others.

In the world that we live in, knowledge always has and will always be an important asset. It makes you a master of the field. If any information is required, you can easily share it with the rest. The options industry is diverse, and there is a lot to be learned regarding it. With each passing day, some new information comes up, which is relevant while trading. You find that you constantly need to keep up with the information that is coming up. This is a field that keeps undergoing regular changes. The interesting thing about it is that these changes that occur are relevant in staying on top of the game while trading. It translates to the fact that what you knew yesterday may not be beneficial today. Essentially, for you to keep growing and sustain the positions that you are in, you will have to acquire knowledge that is relevant to that period you are trading. Primarily, your biggest task involves constantly keeping up with the new information. You could have a plan where you set aside some days to study more about options trading. This venture may appear to be complex to some, especially with the technical terms involved. For some, it may be a little challenging to come along, and therefore, mastering the art might be difficult. The best strategy for amateurs would be gaining the relevant information that will be useful to them while trading options.

2. Start small

We all have big dreams regarding our future. At times, the dreams we have do not allow us to be happy about small beginnings. At times, we want to get to certain points badly, and we forget that it is a process. Most of the success stories that we get often have the value of perseverance attached to them. You will find that the individuals never gave up on their dreams, which is why they got to the point where they are today. We also aim for the skies as they did and hope that we will get where they are. As a beginner in the day trading industry, you have certain plans. Perhaps, you have already pictured yourself as a multi-millionaire who owns properties across the world. You have some occasional fantasies of traveling to your dream destinations and having a good time. Well, such dreams are amazing, and everyone has such dreams once in a while, well, at least before they make it. There is nothing wrong with having those big and incredible dreams. The mistake that we make is thinking that we get them from a silver platter unless it's out of an inheritance. You have to work hard and smart to get what you want. In this case, to make it in the options industry, you will have to be committed to learning, and at the same time, ensure that you have the right tips to succeed. In addition, you have to delight in humble beginnings.

Some people think that if they invest using a lot of cash, they will equally get a lot of profits. Well, that is possible if you properly consider all the factors that surround the trade and if you manage to trade accordingly. To have successful trades, you need to consider a variety of factors. For instance, you will have to ensure that you know the best strategies to utilize, as well as create a well-written trading plan. You also need proper timing while carrying out different trades and diverse knowledge of trading. All these factors, when properly considered, will ensure that you have a successful time while trading. In case you invest heavily without putting all these factors into consideration, you will end up regretting the choices that you made. Initially, you may not be able to know all the tricks that you need for a successful trade. This will pose a challenge, and hence, it is advisable that you avoid taking great risks when you have little knowledge. In this case, you would rather start small and keep learning as you continue. You find that even with a small investment, you can easily make a profit out of it. The small profits that you make are better than none. At the same time, in case something goes wrong, and you are unable to make a successful trade, the loss incurred will not be as big as the one you would have acquired in case you invested with a lot of finances.

3. *Be realistic about profits*

The main aim of investing is accumulating profits that you get to earn at the end of the day. Investors are constantly looking for new ventures that they can engage in to make a fortune. In the world we live in, money runs most things (if not everything). We live looking for money to spend on different expenses. All our basic needs require money, and for us to live comfortable lives, we are constantly looking for money that we can spend on different things. Getting an investment that gets you the money that you want is the climax of each investor. The trading industry appears to be quite a catch, especially when you master the art and become good at trading. There are individuals who are making millions from this industry on a daily basis. Perhaps you have heard about them, and that is what inspired you to get into the industry. That is a nice move as it shows that you are the kind of person who is open to new opportunities and that whenever they arise, you are fast enough to grasp them. Such an attitude gets you far in the investment industry. It will get you to places and positions that you never imagined. Ideally, this happens when you do it right and manage to conquer the investments that you are dealing with.

The downside of being in this industry is the need to have very high expectations of getting favorable results from the beginning. In this case, you find that you expect that the first investment you make gets back to you, in addition to a huge profit. In the event that this fails to happen, you become frustrated, and you question why you invested in the first place. One of the attributes that will help you as an investor is learning to be patient. While setting the profits that you expect from your investment, you have to consider a variety of things. Having realistic profits will help you avoid the stress that comes from failing to hit the targets that you anticipated. Often, we are victims of counting on unclosed deals. You might be aiming at a certain profit at the end of the trade, so you end up planning ahead regarding how you will use the profits. In case you fail to get the profits that you were aiming for, you become frustrated. The best thing is always avoiding having unrealistic targets. It will also help you avoid having unrealistic dreams attached to those profits. Well, it is not bad having big dreams; the challenge comes when you try to reach beyond your limit, and hence, you end up being frustrated. With a small investment, you can set realistic profits that are within the investment made. At times, having

74

realistic profits helps you avoid making trading mistakes. You find that you are more informed and make wise trading decisions that result in successful trades.

4. *Set aside your time and money*

As you trade, you need to invest in your time and money. While trading options is a flexible industry that does not need much of your time, you need to invest your time at the beginning of your trading career. Previously, I have mentioned the importance of having the required knowledge. To gain this knowledge, you need to spare some of your time to access the information. You may decide that you spend an hour each day sharpening your skills and knowledge on trading options. There are many sources of trading information that you can utilize. Currently, we have organizations and individuals offering some training in the options industry. One can take advantage of such opportunities to learn more concerning trading options. Due to the technicalities involved, it might be difficult for some to gain the knowledge required within a short period of time. It might take a process before they get to a point where they are confident enough that they can engage in a trade. For such people, they have to spare some of their time ensuring that they become better at the skill, even for them to earn from it. Knowledge is a powerful fighting tool. It gives you a firm foundation and helps you achieve what you are fighting so hard to get. Having full information regarding the field that you are operating in can easily make you a master of the game.

Having set aside some of your time to learn more, the next things that you need to set aside is money. It interests me whenever I come across people who are not willing to spend in order to earn. The whole thought on its own is deceptive. There is no way that you can earn a profit without spending some of your money to get it. Some businessmen have learned this misguided thought and used it to their advantage. You might come across some ventures that claim to be free, and you are promised some money at the end of the day. Afterward, you come to learn that it was a scam, yet you invested your time trying to learn it or trying to do what is expected of you. At the end of the day, you end up being frustrated because you didn't get the $1000 that the website promised. Well, I don't think any investor can come up with a scheme where they give money to random strangers. Unless they have decided to be charitable, that won't happen. If it is something that earns you money, there has to be an exchange of services, goods, or money that is meant for investing. If none of these three factors are involved, it is difficult to get to earn from the venture. When you decide to trade options, you have to be willing to set aside a portion of your investment to go into trading. After a successful trade, you can expect your money.

Trade Management

In trade management, the trader has to come up with activities that minimize risks and increase the chances of earning a profit. Every trader needs trade management. This is a feature that ensures that your trades are successful and that you are able to minimize your chances of incurring a loss. As you trade, you need to decide the type of trade you wish you engage in, the amount of money you are willing to spend in a trade, the risks involved, and the challenges that you are likely to face. And then you need to come up with a proper trading plan. Among the different ventures, the management determines how well the venture is likely to perform. In business, competition is the order of the day. There will always be someone who is doing better than you are, and the only thing that will be expected of you is ensuring that you perform better than them. In an organization set up, the management in charge acts as the heartbeat of the organization. You find that for it to survive, it needs strong leadership in the different managerial positions. Any slight set back can make the organization crumble down faster than it began. We have had very big companies fall down due to poor management. Primarily, the success of any company is determined by how well structured they are in terms of management. In options trading, the management involved determines the success of the trade at the end of the day.

While coming up with a management plan, you need to have a vision. Identify what you want from your trading career and go for it. While trading, you will come across different things that you need to learn, so you can become a better trader. You will have to be well aware of the trading market and how it works. Depending on the brokerage account that you are using, you can easily get the information regarding the trading market. Some brokerage accounts provide graphs and analysis of the market. With proper evaluations, you can easily decide on the best stocks to trade in, and at the same time, you can know the trades to avoid in case you do not want to end up making a loss. Take some time analyzing the patterns taken by most trades. You may decide that there is a constant or recurrent pattern of successful trades at a certain time. On the other hand, it could be a pattern of unsuccessful trades that lead you to frustrations. Evaluate the circumstances resulting in the turnout of events and make proper decisions from that point. The other thing you need to manage is to stop losses. You need to move your stop in a way that it can survive severe changes in the market. This is to ensure that you remain on top as you avoid risks. With the right trade management strategies, you can easily carry out successful trades that you will be proud of in the end.

Position Sizing Strategies

In a position sizing strategy, a trader has to adjust the position contract at the beginning or before a buy order/short trading order. Having the right position sizing strategy can help you come up with better strategies and improve your trading experience. As a trader, you are always looking forward to creating a good portfolio that can grant you some bragging rights. We can equate the portfolio to an academic report card. When in school, we usually get a report showing how well we have scored in the tests provided. It's the report card that can help you know the best-performing students. Even as you apply for a scholarship or any financial aid for your studies, you need to show your capabilities in different fields to the people from whom you are seeking help. In this case, your report card sells you out and makes you stand out among other people. When these people are testing your eligibility to stand a chance at being funded, the report card will majorly impact their decision. Based on their policies and qualifications, they will decide if they will fund you or not. The same applies to the trading industry; our trading portfolios are proof of our success in trading. With a good portfolio, you can easily brag that you are an expert trader. However, you need to maintain your position, for you to keep having a good portfolio that you can easily show off.

There are different position-sizing techniques that you can utilize. They are:

1. *Fixed risk per trade*

   To regulate the capital used per trade, this technique utilizes three variables. The variables considered are a maximum risk, risk per trade, and stop loss. Under the stop loss, there is a limited-stop loss that is allowed per trade. Beyond the set limit, you cannot keep engaging in a stop loss. By doing so, you can easily retain your position.

2. *Fixed dollar amount*

   Your portfolio equity is equally influenced by a number of positions in your portfolio. When the portfolio equity decreases, they decrease, and as they increase, the number of positions equally increases. In this technique, you engage in a fixed number of dollars per new trade.

3. *Volatility based on position sizing*

   The lower the volatility, the lower the risk, and the vice versa is also applicable. For each new underlying asset, you have to access the historical volatility. The number of shares that a trader can enter will be dependent on the volatility of the underlying instrument. When there is high volatility, the shares to be bought will be fewer, and when there is low volatility, more shares can be bought by the trader.

The above techniques will help the trader in position sizing. There are more techniques to be learned that can be useful while trading. As a trader, you need to be open to new information and be committed to learning more. With such an attitude, you will go far in the options industry.

Chapter 9: Risk and Account Management

Three-Step Risk Management Trading Psychology

1. Accept the risk

Almost all the investments that one can engage in have the potential of acquiring a risk. As an options trader, you have to be open to the possibility of coming across risks. At times, when you get to your risk management software, you identify that there is a risk. The first step will involve coming into terms with its existence. Instead of immediately taking action to counter the risk, first, accept that there is a risk. Ideally, risks are not good for business; hence, no one likes coming across them. When they occur, they might not make you walk away, celebrating. Instead, you will be worried that they may interfere with your investment.

On the brighter side, you can make something positive out of the risks incurred. For instance, you may decide to learn from the risks. As a trader, there are several ups and downs that you will come across. The best thing would be utilizing each moment to be a learning lesson where you could turn things around in your favor. As you keep incurring the risks, they are able to shape you and make you a better trader. At times, the risks incurred make you do more than you thought you could. After accepting the risks, it becomes very easy to come up with an appropriate risk management strategy. In the previous chapter, we have discussed the options strategies that you can utilize to make a better trader. Most of the strategies are aimed at minimizing the risk to reduce the chances of incurring a loss. You can utilize them to minimize the possible losses that you can encounter due to the risks incurred.

2. *Come up with ways to manage the risks*

Now that you have already identified the risk, the next step will involve coming up with ways to manage the risk. You will first look into the root cause of the risk, identify the contributing factors as you come up with the best solutions for the situation at hand. Some of the strategies that you can use to tackle the situation happen to be specific, depending on the events surrounding the trade. You find that different trades set up are influenced by different factors and circumstances. These later result in a difference in the way we tackle the situation. At the same time, you find that if you know more about the different options strategies that you can utilize, it becomes easy for you to easily come up with a proper risk management plan.

We can compare this situation with a different scenario. Suppose a soap company realizes that they are suddenly experiencing losses from the items that they are selling. They can send some of their marketers to identify the cause of the situation. These marketers come back with feedback from the users, who have aired out their complaints. Some of the issues raised are that some barely lasts for long, some take time to lather in hard water, irritating when it comes into contact with the skin, and has a bleaching effect on clothes. After the company has listened to the issues raised, they can decide to make a change so that they do not keep losing their clients. In this case, the company has assessed the situation that was placing its business at risk, and they have decided to come up with ways in which they can resolve the situation so they can keep their business. The same applies to trade options. You first access the risk associated with your trade and come up with that best solution for the issue. One mistake that we, at times, make is thinking that the same risk management you utilized in a given trade will work in all the trades that you make. Depending on the circumstances surrounding a type of trade, the methods used might be different. You need to keep learning so as to have a variety of risk management plans that you can use based on the situation you are in and the risks involved. With such an attitude, it will be possible to come up with a good plan.

3. *Exploit the risk management plan*

The final step will involve taking action. In this case, we mean that you fully utilize all your resources for your benefit. In this case, you make your final action toward the task involved. At this point, you have to be careful that you make the right decision and ensure that you do not make a mistake that you will end up regretting. You can decide to keenly evaluate all your options as you come up with the best plan. At the same time, you have to see if you can find other alternatives to use before settling on one. The best thing about having more information is that it allows you to make a wise selection after evaluating all your options. I keep insisting that as a trader, you have to be well informed to make wise decisions.

Like the case of the soap company, at this point, they need to come up with a good solution for the challenges to the user. If they are committed to provide quality and retain their clients, they can decide to tackle each problem with a solution. In the case of causing skin irritation, they can include some protective chemicals or remove the ingredient contributing to the irritation. At the same time, they can decide to regulate the ingredient that causes the bleaching effect, just to ensure that the clothes retain their original color. By solving the problems, they can retain their clients and even get more clients, which will later translate into more profits. As a trader, you can also use this in handling the risks that you encounter. You identify the risk, come up with possible solutions, and, finally, you take action.

Chapter 10: Introduction to Candlesticks

The history of the candlesticks is tied to the Japanese. In the 17th century, they began using technical analysis to trade rice. The Japanese version varied with the US version of technical analysis that was initiated by Charles Dow in 1900. However, despite their differences, they had some similarities. Some of the similarities in the principles included market fluctuation. Also, the underlying value may not be well-represented by the actual price, and the emotions and expectations of the buyers and sellers can influence the market. Another similarity was that the price action is more important than the earnings and news, and the price is a reflection of the known information. Homma, a well-known rice trader from the town of Sakata, is popularly linked to candlestick development. Over the years, his ideas have been modified to create the present candlestick charting that is currently being used.

Formation of Candlesticks

For you to come up with a candlestick, you need data, containing low, high, close, and open values for the time period that you want to display. The body refers to the filled portion of the candlestick, while the long thin lines below and above the body show the low/high range, and they are referred to as wicks and tails or shadows. The lower shadow shows the low, and the upper shadow shows the high. A hollow candlestick is drawn if the stock closes higher than the opening price. The top of the body shows the closing price, and the opening price is at the bottom of the body. Alternatively, when the opening price is higher than the stock while closing, we have a filled candlestick at the top of the body. The top will represent the opening price, as the closing price is represented by the bottom of the body.

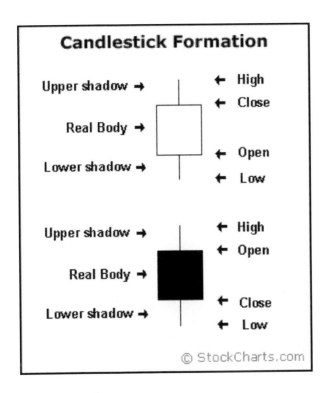

© StockCharts.com

Price Action Mass Psychology

In a speculating market, the price is not dependent on a particular entity. This means that the price is not fixed, and hence, it keeps changing, depending on the different factors that influence it. The price is mainly a consensus between the sellers and the buyers. They keep changing, depending on the circumstances surrounding the trade.

The price action is agreed upon depending on the consensus and mass psychology. As a trader, you do not have control over the mass psychology. What you can do is use the market psychology to make better decisions. Ideally, a good marketer is one that has mastered the art of manipulation. You need to have a good understanding of people's reasoning and know what influences them in making decisions while buying. As a trader, this art can be helpful while carrying out your transactions. Get to study the mood of the situation as you come up with the best strategies to use for you to make successful trades. If you see that the price is continuously moving in one direction, you can decide to engage in the trade if it will give you a better return.

Bullish Candlesticks

The candlesticks have descriptive names like dark cloud cover, three white soldiers, morning star, abandoned baby, and hammer. They are mainly grouped into descriptive names and recognizable patterns. The patterns are created from one to four weeks. The pattern can be used in deciding the future of the price action. In bullish candlesticks, the reversal patterns form in a downward trend. At the same time, the patterns need bullish confirmation. I can site 5 bullish candlestick patterns that offer the strongest reversal signals.

1. *The bullish engulfing*

   It is a two candle reversal pattern where the second candle engulfs the first candle.

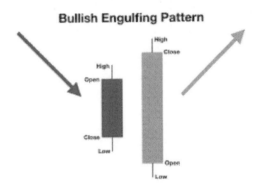

Bullish Engulfing Pattern

2. *The inverted hammer or the hammer*

   It shows an indication that a trend is close to the bottom in a downtrend

Bullish Hammer

3. The piercing line

This is a two candle bullish reversal pattern that occurs in downtrends. It is closely similar to the engulfing pattern.

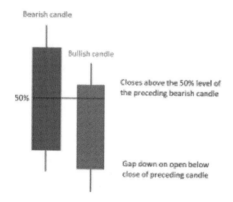

Bearish candle

Bullish candle

Closes above the 50% level of the preceding bearish candle

50%

Gap down on open below close of preceding candle

4. The morning star

The morning star offers a sign of hope and a new beginning. It is made of three candlesticks, including one short-bodied, long white candle, and a long black candle.

Morning Star

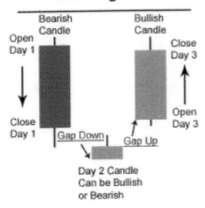

5. *The three white soldiers*

It is observed in price consolidation or after a period of a downtrend. It involves three white candles that move higher with each trading day.

The candles demonstrate an advance in buying pressure.

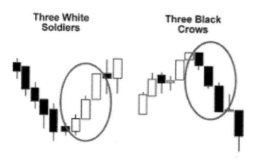

Bearish Candlesticks

The bearish reversal patterns can form in more than one candlestick. Some of the common bearish candlesticks are the bearish abandoned baby, engulfing bearish, evening star, shooting star, dark cloud cover, and Harami bearish. The reversal shows that the selling pressure overwhelms the buying pressure for a day or more. However, it remains unclear if the price will be affected by the selling or lack of buyers. The bearish confirmation is expected within one to three days since the candlestick patterns are short-term.

Indecision Candlesticks

In the price action trading system, we can use some powerful candlestick signals, such as the indecision candlestick. One of the factors that we must consider is that the close price of the candle is closer to the open price. In other words, it should have a small body. Secondly, the body of the candle ought to be centered within the high and low candle range. They also need long wicks that project from each side of the body, around equal lengths. The wicks show that the price either moved up or down during the trade.

Below is an illustration of an indecision candlestick.

The Indecision Candle

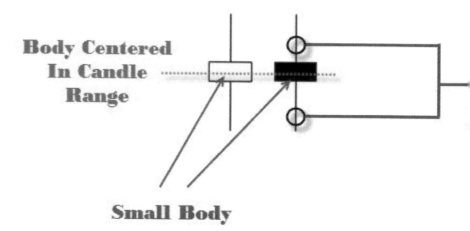

Body Centered In Candle Range

Small Body

Candlestick Patterns

Some candlestick patterns work well, while others do not. As their popularity increases, their reliability has been lowered, especially by hedge funds. Most hedge fund managers utilize software to look for traders looking for high odds, bearish, or bullish outcomes. There are some consistent patterns that keep appearing to give room for short and long-term profit opportunities. Some of the top five candlestick patterns include the three-line strike, two black gapping, three black crows, evening star, and abandoned baby. Mainly, the candlesticks capture the attention of players.

PART FOUR

HOW TO SUCCEED IN DAY TRADING

Chapter 11: Building a Watch List Trading Plan

A trading plan offers a guide on how we carry out our trading activities. It can help you make important trade decisions a trader. Below are some factors that you need to consider while coming up with a trading plan.

1. *Understand your commitment to trading*

   We all have different inspirations that led us to invest in trading options. For instance, you might have a desire to have an extra source of income; another individual might want to become a millionaire and is seeking financial freedom by engaging in different investments. All these individuals have the right dreams, and they should inspire them to succeed at trading options. At times, it is difficult to work hard and give our all in the activities that we are undertaking, and it is, therefore, important to find something that sets the mood and allows us to achieve our goals. You find that any time you feel like giving up, your goals keep you committed to achieving the best out of life. It is very easy to lose hope or to lack faith in our capabilities, especially when we encounter failure. However, these goals make us have something to look forward to each day, regardless of the challenges that we face in life. We are always inspired to do better and become more than we could imagine we would become.

I tend to hold a belief that there is power in writing our goals down. Having a point of reference each day makes it easier to push toward getting what you aim to achieve. For instance, you can have a place where you have written down your goals. You get to ensure that each morning when you wake up, you go through the different goals that you have. At the same time, you have to ensure that you do not give up on your goals when challenges strike. Life, as it is, will not always be a smooth, straight line. It has its own curves and bent areas. At times, you will come across some bumpy roads. There are moments when you will feel like giving up on your dreams, especially when things are not moving as planned. You may encounter a lot of such days while trading. At the beginning of your trading career, you will stumble at one point, but you need to pick yourself up. When such challenges strike, your instant solution should not be to quit. Instead, you should be looking for a way where you can pick yourself up after you stumbled. The good thing about having goals is that they take us back to our starting point. You get an understanding of why you started, and it inspires you to keep pushing. If you are a beginner or if you are already trading, part of the solution of coming up with a trading plan involves having some goals that you look forward to achieving.

2. Assess your skills

While coming up with a trading plan, it is advisable that you assess your skills. Depending on the time you have spent trading and your years of experience, you may have different trading skills. Normally, if you are a beginner, your skills are incomparable with an expert who has been in the game for long. You find that there is some information that you might not be aware of, but the other individual is well informed. This difference in the skills attained also portrays a difference in the amount of money that you earn from the different trades. While coming up with a trading plan, be familiar with your skills and abilities. This assessment helps you in making numerous trade decisions. For instance, as a beginner, you should avoid engaging in multiple trades. The reason behind this decision results from the fact that you might not be fully aware of how to trade. Your skills are limited, and hence, taking up bigger challenges may not turn out so well for you. At the same time, patience is necessary. You do not expect that you will immediately start earning six-figure incomes at the beginning. One must be willing to take simple steps before they can proceed to much bigger steps. After all, the journey of a thousand miles begins with a single step. While at it, you should be gracious enough to believe in the steps that you take.

While assessing your skills, you can also set some realistic goals. At times, our huge expectations deceive us into setting goals that we cannot achieve. The majority of the traders are victims of making such mistakes. To avoid getting frustrated when you fail to hit your target, it is best if you classify your goals in different categories. For instance, you might be having some short-term and long-term goals. For your short-terms goals, you write down some things that are easily achievable and, at the same time, make sure that they are realistic. For example, if I bought the underlying stock at $19, I would expect to sell at $29 and get a profit of $10. Such a plan is very realistic and practical. One can easily achieve such a trade. With regard to the long-term goals, this is where you document your ambitions. In case you want to travel the world, own a mansion, and buy your dream car, your strategies today will determined such goals in the future. At this point, you are allowed to give more when it comes to your choices. This is a safe space to write plans for your future. After writing them down, make sure that they set the pace for you. In this case, any trade that you make should be inspired by the goals that you have. Skills assessment can be effective in gaining more knowledge. Once you discover that you are not as skilled as you ought to be, it makes you inspired to learn more.

3. *Having a trading journal*

If you like journaling like I do, having a journal should not be a debatable issue. It comes automatically, and it goes without saying. I tend to believe that things become more real when written on paper. When the pen connects with the book and sends a message to inspire by the writer, it's all magic altogether. Journaling helps us express our ideas and goals that we want to achieve. For instance, earlier on, I mentioned that we should write down our goals. I went ahead to explain how having them written down helps us work hard toward achieving them. Any time you get to open your journal, you get to see the various goals that you have, and it, in turn, inspires you to do more. Life will, at times, pose its own challenges, and we may forget what we want out of it; therefore, having a constant reminder of why we are living makes the whole difference. As you educate yourself more about day trading, it is good to note down some of the points that you have picked up while reading. If you are a slow learner, this is something that will help boost your learning process and make things easier for you. Documenting helps in creating some emphasis on the information acquired. You find that you easily understand and recall what you read.

Having a journal can also help you in tracking your progress. For instance, you can record the number of trades that you have made in a day. While recording, include some information and details regarding the trade. State if you made a profit or a loss. You can go ahead to include some of the strategies that you used in the trade. While at it, ensure that you document the time when the trade took place. With this information, there is a lot that you can learn. You can identify certain trading patterns that often result in successful trades. While at it, you will identify the strategies that work and those that do not. On the other hand, you may determine the best time to conduct a trade and when to avoid engaging in a trade. With the number of trades that you have previously done, you can set a trade limit. When you realize that your trades are moving as expected, you can keep having the same trend. Still, if you realize that you are making more losses than profits, then that can act as a red flag to avoid engaging in more trades. Each information that we pick from the journals that we make is essential in building our trading life. There is always something to learn from each move that we make. Writing down different trade details can help us avoid making trading mistakes. For instance, it is very easy to forget the expiration date or time, but with a journal, it is difficult to miss out on such dates.

4. Risk management skills

There are different risks that you will experience while trading. There are some instances where you will feel as if you are placing a bet. In such moments, your trade is entirely dependent on luck. You find that there are a lot of uncertainties involved, which increase the chance of either getting a profit or ending up with a loss. While both situations are possible at that instance, it is very important to have some risk management skills. The option strategies that we use in different trades happen to be major in risk management. I have discussed some of these strategies in the previous chapters to ensure that you get a smooth trading experience. You find that the option strategies emphasize minimizing the risks as you maximize the profits. Risks, if not properly handled, can sabotage the whole investment scheme. You might find that you are more invested in trading without properly evaluating all the risks that are involved; it becomes easy to make a loss. In such an instance, you get to miss out on major details that you need to have at your tips. As a result, you get in a trade that is exposed to numerous risks, and you have no way to get out of it; hence, it ends up in a loss. To avoid exposing yourself to risks while trading, it is important that you know all the options strategies that you can utilize.

When it comes to option strategies, get as much information as possible. The trading industry is swiftly diversifying, and new options strategies keep coming up on a daily basis. One needs to keep up with the daily changes for them to ensure that they remain competitive. For some, getting this becomes a big struggle, and hence, they fail to make progress while trading. Well, the trading industry is an interesting space. The more you are willing to learn and sharpen your skills, the more things become manageable and easier to handle. With a little rest or slight shift of focus, you may find yourself at a position you would not have imagined yourself to be in. As you get in the trading industry, one needs to be well prepared for the risks that they will encounter. Well, like any other investment out there, we have some risks involved while trading options. An individual's ability to come up with proper risk management skills keeps them relevant in the game. Some people become a bit skeptical about engaging in a trade because of the risks involved. I'm afraid that such people cannot make it in the investment world. There is no single venture that will have zero risks. In a business or investment, there are both internal and external factors influencing the success of the business. Some of these factors can pose a risk to the venture, thus exposing it to the possibility of encountering a loss. One needs to have proper risk management skills that are effective in such incidences.

5. *Determine the amount of money you wish to invest*
The amount of money an individual uses while trading has remained a topic under debate for a long period of time. We seem to have mixed

reactions on what should be spent and what we should avoid spending. From my own perspective, as a beginner, you should have some limits on the amount of money that you spend. Taking into consideration that you are still learning and trying to find your foot in the industry, taking big risks may not be a wise move. At the same time, you want to go low on your budget to ensure that you do not make losses that you cannot recover from. I feel like I would write an entire book on the importance of having a budget and how it can be a real lifesaver. Spending on things that you had not budgeted for is always an unwise move. It makes us remain at a point of stagnation, and we rarely make an impact in our lives. While conducting multiple trades, we, at times, end up spending money that we had not planned for. This mainly occurs while trying to cover up for a previous trade that ended up in a loss. You trade again, hoping that it will cover for the previous trade and that you will make more profit, so you will not have to suffer due to the previous loss.

We are constantly being advised not to spend more than we can afford to lose. For instance, if you had $ 100, making a $90 investment would be a huge risk to take. With such an amount, your investment should not be beyond $50. At times, we listen to different stories of individuals who did not struggle to make a fortune. You end up getting very inspire and excited, which can, at times, cause you to count your chicks before they hatch. To avoid finding yourself in such incidences, it is important that you do not approach any investment with huge expectations. The plans that you have in mind may fail to come into action, which, in turn, results in huge frustrations. While it is healthy to have big dreams and to want more out of life, you need to minimize your expectations to a realistic level. While discussing the point on setting goals, I have explained the essence of having both short-term and long-term goals. For the short term goals, we have a more realistic approach, while in the long-term goals, we are allowed to stretch our minds beyond our own expectations and imaginations. As an amateur trader, you need to minimize the amount of money that you spend while trading. Always ensure that if the trade does not move as planned, you will be in a position to accept the outcome. As you keep advancing and getting better at trading, you can start committing more money to it.

6. *Know when to exit or enter a trade*

As a trader, you need to learn when to enter a trade and when to exit a trade. Interestingly, most of us have mastered the art of entering a trade, but few of us know when to exit. You find that the trade was doing really well at the beginning, but because we failed to identify when to quit, we end up experiencing a loss. The same commitment we have while engaging in a trade should be the same commitment that we should apply while exiting. There are some red flags that can easily point out when it is time to exit. If one is careful enough, they cannot fail to notice some of these red flags. While trading, one needs to be keen, any slight shift or sudden occurrence should be easily detectable before it sabotages your investment.

Instead of being focused on identifying buying signals, we also need to shift to being focused on noting exit signals. This focus will save a lot of traders from making huge trading mistakes. At the same time, we need to identify when to take a break from trading. You might be encountering a series of losses from all the trades that you engage in. Once you realize such a sequence, it should act as an alarm for you to stop trading.

You can take some time off to establish what it is that you are doing wrong while trading. At this point, you can evaluate the different trades that you have made and realize where you went wrong. At this point, there is a lot that you can learn from previous mistakes. You may find that the strategies that you used were a problem, and therefore, it can offer a chance to rectify some of the mistakes that you made. Often, when you make a series of mistakes, you will realize that you failed to have the relevant information. It might narrow down to embracing that you need to learn the areas where you failed and making a difference after learning

114

how to make a change. Even as we emphasize on having an exit plan, it is equally important to know when to get in a trade. With the help of a journal, you can easily identify the best time to get in a trade. In a journal, you get to document all the events surrounding the trades that you make. From the things that you have written down, one can easily come up with a trading pattern that they can utilize to determine the best time to engage in a trade.

With the above information, I believe that you can easily come up with a trading plan. All you need to do is to put all these factors into consideration while planning. A trader with a trading plan is at a more advantage than one without. It's like exploring a new place without a map; you end up getting lost and make it impossible to find your way.

7. *Select the right broker*

Be careful while selecting the right broker through which you carry out your trade. This process is essential since there are many brokers currently.

Some of which end up being scams, and you lose your money before you even invest. At times, we are quick to take action and fail to analyze the various steps that we take. So we end up making rash decisions that we regret later on. The process of looking for a suitable broker is very crucial since it determines how your investment turns out. Ideally, any individual would like investing in a place where their investment is well protected, and they are guaranteed great returns at the end of it all. As the market grows and expands, there are a lot of emerging brokers. Some have good intentions, while others are after stealing people's money. As an investor, you need to be careful so that you can find a legit broker. In the current digital space, there are amazing things that one can do with the help of the internet and various search engines. With a single click, you can discover the best brokers in the swing trading market based on the information provided. You can also use referrals to get a good broker. It is also advisable that you access this information from individuals who have dealt with those brokers. In the book, I have mentioned some of the factors that you can consider while selecting the best broker to engage with.

You find that the type of brokerage account that you have influences the investment that you make. As you decide to engage in day trading, you need to ensure that you get a trader who meets your demands and ensures that they can secure your investment. The process of selecting the best brokerage account is very critical, yet we tend to ignore it most of the time. This is a place where you are investing your finances, so you have to ensure that you make wise decisions. If you make a wrong decision and land with a broker who does not help you in realizing your dream, you will end up with major regrets. On the other hand, you will lose the money that you have worked so hard to get so you could invest.

8. *The time to trade*

The way we do things requires order and precision. One of the tricks that successful people make in life is being very particular with time. The time factor has been a topic regularly associated with matters of success. You are probably wondering about the essence of proper timing when it comes to day trading. Well, as you trade, you will find out that there are certain times the trades have a high likelihood of earning a profit, and, at other times, you end up with a loss. One of the ways you can figure this out is through tracking your progress. If you have a journal where you note down the trades you make and provide the timestamps, it could be an added advantage. You get to analyze the different trades that you have made and see the duration of time within which you made the different trades. From your findings, you can come up with the time when you can place your trades. One of the beautiful things about trading is that you trade within your convenience. At times, we get too comfortable and fail to observe a number of things, such as time, and end up making a loss. It is important to stay keen, especially on matters on the time you trade

9. *Decide on the number of trades to use while evaluating your performance*

For an individual to keep engaging in day trading, they need to have good performance. How one performs shows the wins and losses that they have encountered. If you keep losing your finances, then that would not be a good venture to keep investing in. keeping track ensures that you make the right choices and helps you know how far you are moving. It is important to regularly track your performance. You can decide on the number of trades to use based on the period you have traded. For instance, you might have traded for a year and done 24 trades in that year. This information points out that you have made at least an average of 2 trades in a month. With this information, you can decide to use at least 4 trades that you carry out in 2 months to track your performance. You can avoid using many trades at once since they may not provide accurate information. The best analysis comes from carrying out an evaluation of the most recent trades. Based on your findings, you get to know the best way to invest.

10.   Identify stocks to trade

Knowing the best stocks is beneficial as it influences the profits you will earn at the end of the day. You have the potential to make high returns or make losses. This possibility is influenced by a number of decisions that you make while trading. Identifying the best stock to engage in happens to be one of the decisions that you need to make. While carrying out this process, try to avoid recently introduced stocks. Lack of experience can pose a challenge to a beginner in the day trading industry. Try looking for the stocks that have had a longer time in the market. Such can guarantee the potential of earning returns. In the process of searching for the best stocks to trade, take some time to analyze the stock market to see the performance of the different stocks. Invest in those that show consistency in their performance; such trades have a high likelihood of earning profits. Remember to take your time and not to rush in making conclusions. Selecting the most suitable stocks is a crucial process while participating.

Chapter 12: Next Steps for Beginner Traders

The 7 Essentials for Day Trading

1. Acquire Knowledge

While trading, having the right information is critical in ensuring your trading success. Most people engage in trade with little information and end up regretting their choices after they have encountered losses. You do not have to learn from your own mistakes for you to start doing things right. At times, it is good to learn from others and pick up some lessons without having to experience them on your own. Well, we constantly speak of how powerful knowledge is, but we rarely take time to gain more knowledge. If you have recently started trading, it is important that you learn to embrace learning and gaining the necessary information. There is a lot of learning that you will need before you master the art of trading. In this book, you will find that most of my emphasis is on learning. I know that you cannot go far if you have not mastered what you are doing. For you to succeed, there are a lot of factors that are involved; however, in trading, learning is the most important factor. The difference between a novice trader and an expert comes in the information that they hold. Most people believe that knowledge goes with years of experience. However, I fail to agree with such beliefs. One can be in an industry for long and fail to learn, and at the same time, one could have recently joined, yet their commitment to learning sets them apart. It all goes with how willing we are to gain knowledge.

You are probably wondering which avenues you can use to learn more about trading. It is amazing that you are already utilizing one of the methods that involve reading books. In the digital world that we are in currently, the internet has been one place where we can derive practically any information. There is a lot of information that we can get from different websites, blogs, journals, and social media platforms. As a disciplined individual, you may decide to spare a few hours of your time learning. You can start small with a few minutes as you advance to gaining more knowledge and applying them to your strategies. While on this journey, you will face some challenges. You may not feel inspired to work hard each day, and thus, you may end up not reading. You have to come up with ways in which you can feel inspired on such days. At times, it will demand that you acquire discipline that pushes you to act accordingly. While at it, also avoid putting too much pressure on yourself. It may take some time to come around some things, and you have to understand that there is no harm in that. You can also acquire information from attending training that majors in educating on options trading. There is plenty of information that you can pick up from such meetings, and this information will be useful in making you a better trader.

2. Decide the Amount of Capital to Spend

In most instances, we fail to discuss the amount of money we need to spend while trading. The majority of the traders begin trading, not knowing the importance of setting a budget. At times, we engage in more than we can afford or less than we can afford. You would rather spend less than what you have than spend more than you have. Sadly, the majority end up using more than they can afford to lose. As you decide to engage in options trading, it is important that you come up with a budget. The budget is not meant to restrict you, but it is meant to help you avoid making trading mistakes that you will regret later on, especially if a trade does not turn out as you would have expected. Many traders are consumed in the idea of spending more to earn more, which may not always be the case. You can still earn from a small investment, depending on the strategy that you use while trading. At the same time, you can encounter a loss and lose all the money that you had invested. In such situations, it would be better if you made a small investment instead. If you are a beginner, try to avoid starting with a huge investment. Assuming that at that point, you do not know much. It would be best if you started small and later advanced to huge investments.

At times, we get to a point where we encounter a series of wins in the trades that we make. In such situations, it might be tempting to engage in trading in huge amounts, especially since one is confident that the trade will be successful. You end up reinvesting in one trade all the money you have acquired in previous trades. Things fail to go as planned, and you end up losing all your earnings. Such a move is very risky to take and can leave you regretting your move, especially if it fails to go as planned. When such incidences occur, you get to understand the importance of not placing your eggs in one basket. The losses can be major and damaging to the individual. This incidence can result in some suicidal thoughts among some people and, at times, anxiety and trauma in some. As a trader, you need to avoid getting in such situations. One the other hand, some people decide to spread their capital across different stocks. They do this hoping that in case one fails, they will still earn from the others. When you do this without having the right strategies in place, you might end up regretting your decision, especially when you encounter a loss. Avoid getting yourself in such situations by making decisions that you are sure about. For instance, when you decide to trade in that manner, make sure that you have a proper plan and that you have the right strategies to succeed in the trade.

3. Create a Trading Plan

In the previous chapter, we have discussed things that one should consider while coming up with a trading plan. A plan is essential to a trader since it provides a sense of direction. Having a good plan can help you achieve success while trading, and it can place you in a better position as compared to an individual who lacks a plan. Most of the successful traders will tell you that they had plans that inspired them while trading and helped them scale to bigger height. Success is not something that comes instantly. We have to properly plan for it and ensure that we have put up measures that can guarantee that we get to the point that we want in life. At times, it is very easy to forget why we started. Thus, we need a plan that shows our goals. Such goals give us something to live for and inspire us to give our best in what we do. In spite of the challenges that we face, we feel motivated to keep pushing and to keep trying. Without inspiration, it is difficult to succeed and to push to greater heights. We get comfortable in situations that we should not get comfortable with, and this results in stagnation. It is about time that we learn to stay out of a limited mentality and learn to expand our thoughts and ideas on how to

126

live best. This brings us in a situation of motivating ourselves to do more in life.

A plan can also help in coming up with a budget and deciding the number of trades we engage in per day. We know some individuals who are struggling with overtrading, and it becomes something that they cannot control or stop. The thought of wanting to get more money has led many in a lot of trading mistakes that they keep regretting later when they lose the money that they invested. You find that even after making a loss in a given trade, you keep trading, hoping to recover in the other trades. Without the right trading strategies and lack of a proper plan, you end up making a loss in the other trades. Such an incidence can be frustrating to a trader. No one likes making losses, and when it happens, you feel sad about the whole situation. With a good trading plan, you can easily decide on the number of trades you can make in a day. Once you have reached the limit, you should be disciplined enough to avoid engaging in more trades. This points out the importance of discipline while trading. At the same time, a plan can help you track your progress. If you are the type of trader who keeps a journal and you document every move you make while trading, it becomes easy to track your progress. You can easily identify what you are doing right and what you are doing wrong.

4. *Have the Right Trading Strategies*

Among the previous chapters, I have discussed the various trading strategies. While trading, you need to come up with approaches that can guarantee you trading success. One of the ways to ensure that you become a trading expert is to have the information at the tips of your fingers. In this case, ensure that you familiarize yourself with all the trading strategies that are useful to a trader. At times, this is not the kind of information that you learn in one sitting. It requires commitment and dedication while mastering the art. For some, they learn from the mistakes that they make while trading. You might have utilized a certain strategy that failed to work, and hence, you note the circumstances of the trade and note why the strategy did not work. Documenting such will help you avoid making the same mistake another time. At the same time, you can also learn from strategies that worked through the same formula. After a successful trade, note all of the underlying factors that contributed to your success, and you have to be willing to utilize them another time. Each process involved while trading offers a chance to learn more. As a wise trader, you should be ready to learn at all times and ensure that you are willing to improve at all times. The journey may not be as smooth as we expect it to be. However, with the will and determination to learn, it becomes possible to achieve the goals that we hold.

One challenge that some traders face is thinking that the strategies that they know will always work for them. As more people join the trading industry, the market is expanding. With its growth, the market hosts new things that constantly comes up. When this happens, it means that we need to be in line with the changes that are occurring. Some of these changes are in the strategies that we utilize while trading. You find that an approach that you used 5 months ago may not work for you in recent trade. In such situations, you need to remain open to acquire new information. It means that, as a trader, learning is one of the attributes that you require. Each day presents its own challenges, and we have to come up with the right solutions that help us become better. The strategies used do not only focus on how to conduct a trade but also how to prepare for a trade. As a trader, you need to have a strategy on the best time to carry out a trade and how to prepare for it. Some of the information that you need to make this happen may not be learned from the book. You will need to go the extra mile in some situations for you to get to the point you desire. From previous trading patterns, there is a lot that you can pick up that can transform the way you trade. You need to break free from the idea that someone has to give you information and instead acquire the information on your own.

5. Have a Mentor

Having a mentor will create a difference in your day trading journey. As an investor, you may have a financial planner or a life coach, but do you have a trading mentor? The same way you invest in having a better life and properly utilizing your earnings should be the same way you invest in trading. It is important to note that day trading is like any investment; hence, you have to place certain mechanisms to ensure that you succeed. Truth be told, trading options is not a walk in the park for all traders. For some, it is difficult to come by all the technical terms involved, and this, in turn, makes the investment to suffer from low or no returns. Ideally, no one engages in an investment with the intention of failing at some point. You mainly aim to become successful in the trades you make for you to be proud of what you have achieved so far. Having a mentor does not mean that you are weak on your own. It means that you are strong enough to acknowledge that you need guidance to grow and move further than where you are currently. It is a brilliant move to have such an acknowledgment. A mentor should help in accelerating the different processes. Basically, if you were to get somewhere with 30 steps, with the help of a mentor, you get there with 15 steps.

The challenge most people are facing is paying for mentorship services. You might feel as if you have already spent your money on the investment, and you do not understand why you should pay more for the investment. Having such a thought is completely normal, especially since some money is involved, and at the same time, you are clouded with uncertainties whether you are going to make it or not. Well, from my perspective, you would rather invest in a mentor. When you decide to look for a mentor, make sure that is it someone who is already making it in the industry. Such people have encountered the loopholes involved and have learned how to come up with ways on how they can overcome them. They have also studied the different trading patterns, and therefore, they can offer sound advice on the best time to trade. On the other hand, they have identified the strategies that work for different trades and can easily help you come up with a trading plan. The main task that mentors give to their followers is ensuring that you get to certain positions in life faster than they got there. Instead of taking the stress of learning all these things on your own, a mentor makes it fast, and you get to earn your returns at a fast rate. Before engaging anyone as a mentor, run a background check. Look if you can identify their achievements. In case they mentor more people, look at the reviews that they get to ensure that you land a good mentor.

6. Set Some Goals

Once you decide to invest in day trading, establish some goals that would motivate you to keep investing regularly. There are some days when you will feel like you made the wrong decision, and you may be tempted to quit. On some days, your strategies in trading may not move as you would expect, which will make you feel demotivated to push further. Having goals changes the whole mood. They give you something to look forward to. This means that regardless of the challenges that you face, you always feel inspired to do better, and even when you feel like giving up, you find a reason to keep pushing. Waking up every morning, feeling motivated by what you do, may appear to be a hassle for some. You find that it is like you are forcing yourself to get in the mood to succeed, and you are barely making a difference in your life. When you decide to trade, learn to love what you do. The passion that you develop makes the whole process easier and manageable. Most traders are completely uninspired by what they do. Some start trading simply because they need to invest and grow their money. With such an attitude, learning becomes difficult, and it also translates to the results that you get.

133

For instance, you remain at the same point while starting, and you barely make progress. This happens mainly because you are uninspired.

It is important that you align your investment with passion. Develop some love for trading. When you learn to do this, it becomes easier for you to trade. Lack of motivation will make your investment a complete loss. You will, at times, have to set the mood on your own for you to work at what you are doing. Aside from the intention of investing to make money, one needs to learn how to love the venture they have invested in. Most people fail because they do not have any attachment to what they do. This makes it difficult to come up with strategies and plans that can help them succeed. As a result, we remain at one point for long, and we barely make progress. Failing from such circumstances has resulted in many people quitting at their first loss. As we invest the money, we need to go the extra mile in making sure that we find something else to live for. For instance, you can show more interest in learning more about day trading. While learning, you may develop certain likings that were not previously present. However, if you find that you have no interest in engaging in trading, it would be best if you avoided it. If you go ahead with trading, you will be sailing in a ship that you are sure will capsize before getting to its final destination. Sadly, most people do not address this issue, and, therefore, people regret it later on after the damage is done.

7. Start Small

The biggest challenge with day trading is that most people engage in trade with huge expectations of becoming rich within a short time. We are clouded with the fantasies of earning a fortune overnight, and we end up feeling frustrated when things do not go as we planned. We have to come into terms with the fact that trading is not a "get rich fast" scheme. We know some people who have been fortunate enough to earn a lot within a short period, but not everyone gets lucky. There are some who are still in the same position where they started. This mainly occurs when an individual fails to properly understand the mechanisms involved while trading. Such mechanisms involve trading strategies, trading plans, trading patterns, and how to conduct successful trades. There is no rocket science involve while learning some things. As long as you are committed and willing to learn, there is nothing that can stop you from acquiring the information. You can decide to commit some of your time to learn and sharpen your skills. With time, you master the art and become an expert. In most cases, you find people setting high targets that seem unachievable, yet they anticipate getting to those levels. As a trader, it is important that you set realistic goals. For instance, with a small investment, set an amount that is slightly higher than what you invest in with half profit or slightly more than what you spent.

At the same time, it is also important to appreciate small wins. It is out of earning small that you eventually start earning big. Every successful person today had a starting point. If they had given up on themselves when they were just getting started, they would not be where they are today. Your growth might be gradual, but you need to trust that you will eventually get to the point where you aspire to be. A small part on your back after little progress will not harm you; instead, it will encourage you to do better than you did previously. At times, you have to be your own cheerleader for you to do more and achieve more. You will not always have people applauding the good work that you are doing, which is why you need to learn how to appreciate yourself. When you trade and earn a profit, no matter how small, learn to appreciate it. Gratitude has a magical way of creating room for more achievements. As you keep trading, you get to learn more tricks and strategies that you can utilize to keep having more successful trade in the future. While starting small, learn to limit the number of trades that you make in a day. If you are a beginner, one or two trades are enough to kick start your trading journey. You may feel excited, and this may tempt you to conduct more trades than you can handle. Therefore, you should avoid making such decisions.

Chapter 13: Mistakes People Make While Trading and How to Avoid Them

Lack of a Plan

While trading, it is important that you have a plan. A plan acts as a compass direction while trading; it shows you the move that you should take to ensure that it is a wise trade decision. In a plan, we have different goals while trading. Some of these goals make our investment in day trading worth our while. They give us hope to achieve more out of life and, at the same time, inspire us to push beyond our abilities. A person's failure to create a plan results in failure. You find that you make investments without properly evaluating all the underlying factors. In case there are some risks involved, you find that you are not aware of them. In turn, these risks exposed you to the possibility of encountering a loss. When such incidences occur, you are not well-prepared with risk management strategies since you failed to have a plan. It goes without saying that a plan will help you achieve a lot in the trading industry. Most of the time, it provides a bearing for the direction that one is taking while trading.

The biggest challenge comes when you are a beginner, and you do not know much about trading. At that point, it is very easy to make a mistake. Any slight move that you take matters and has a big impact on your future. A single move can either sabotage what you have built for years or make you stronger than what you were before. We have seen people succeed at trading, and then, at one point, they lose all that they have worked hard to build. Your success in this industry is dependent on the plans that you have regarding your trading future. Any slight mistake will cause you to go down faster than you could climb up. As you trade, you may come to a point where you encounter a series of wins. Such incidences make you feel confident in trading, and, at some point, you may be deceived to think that you can easily achieve success. At that point, you may decide to do away with having a plan. Such simple decisions can make a huge change in your trading, and you end up making a loss that you may not be able to recover from.

Trading to Cover up for Previous Losses

Most traders are victims of this strategy. After conducting your daily trades, things may not move as planned. You find that you might have expected to get a profit out of the trades made, but instead, you end up with a loss. To cover up for the losses, you decide to engage in another trade, hoping that things will be different. Contrary to your expectations, you end up encountering more losses than you would have imagined. It gets worse if you spent more money on that investment as compared to the previous investments. You get to a situation where you are full of regrets due to the wrong decision that you made. It is important to note that rushed decisions barely lead to anything good. In most cases, they end up in sabotage, and you may not be able to recover from some of these incidences. We ought to learn that two wrongs do not make a right. Once you have made a mistake, the first step does not involve bouncing back to the same thing that caused you to make a mistake. You need to calm down and identify where you went wrong and start reorganizing from that point.

At times, we keep trading even after we make losses because we are in denial. You find that you are in a phase where you find it difficult to admit that you can make a mistake. These difficulties, at times, arise due to the fact that we have high expectations. Anything that does not lead us to achieve the dreams we created for ourselves automatically makes us regret the decisions that we made. At that point, one becomes frustrated since things are not moving as planned. Instead of taking some time off to realize where you went wrong in the previous trade, you immediately engage in another without carefully thinking it through. This is perhaps one of the biggest mistakes that most traders make. While it is good to have big dreams and ambitions, it is important that you do not make wrong decisions while trying so hard to achieve some of these dreams. Well, since the whole point of investing is earning more from the investments that we make, it may not always be the case. There are some days when we will encounter some losses, and they should not lead us in making rush decisions.

Overtrading

As a beginner, you may have started trading with huge expectations. You have this big dream of becoming an overnight success. You decide to invest heavily in your trades, especially after hearing what other traders are earning out of trading. Ideally, it is healthy to have self-belief and imagine that you, too, can get to the point that other investors have reached. While at it, it is essential that you have practical dreams that are achievable. Some people have managed to sell out the idea that trading is an easy task that can result in earning within minutes. However, many people start trading and end up with huge frustrations when they fail to achieve their dreams as fast as experts. You find that with the excitement of engaging in trading, you end up engaging in multiple trades as a way to earn quick money. In this instance, most trade executions are not carefully planned; they are randomly selected. This means that you do not take time to come up with the right strategies to succeed in the different trades, and eventually, you end up losing.

At the same time, we have individuals who spread their risks across different trades. You are uncertain if you will end up making a loss or a profit. In this instance, you decide to spread your risks so that regardless of how the trade goes, you will not experience a total loss. In the beginning, this looks like an attractive strategy, and it almost feels like it is impossible to make a complete loss. However, you should remember that you are taking a gamble. This means that you can either earn a loss or a profit in both situations. It might occur that you experience a loss in all the investments that you made. In this case, that strategy will not benefit you in any way, especially since you still encounter a loss at the end. While coming up with the decision to conduct multiple trades, you need to be open to the idea that anything can happen. At the same time, you need to be well aware of the different option strategies that you can utilize while carrying out different trades. This allows you to remain focused and that you note some red flags before you end up making certain mistakes.

The Belief That a Big Investment Leads to Profits

Some people tend to have a misplaced belief that they need to make a big investment for them to earn a profit. This belief has caused a lot of individuals to make numerous mistakes while trading. we have had people invest a huge amount of their earnings, only to end up making a huge loss. For instance, you have $100 in your account, and you end up investing $90. With such an investment decision, you cannot afford to make a loss. Any wrong move can result in sabotage and make you lose what you worked so hard to get. At this point, with such an amount, you may end up feeling depressed after you have made a loss. Remaining with $10 can be challenging, especially considering that you had more, yet you lost it from making a trading mistake.

At this point, it is important that we learn to avoid placing all our eggs on one basket. In case of an accident, we may end up losing all the eggs and have none that is spared.

If you are a beginner, you should learn the importance of starting small. We find that most beginners are suffering from such decisions. You find that with the excitement of starting a new investment, you tend to overspend. This causes you to spend much of your time and energy on the new investment, and you barely take time to think things through. You end up making rash decisions that prove to be wrong later on, especially when things do not work in your favor. After experiencing a loss, you get to the point of self-realization that the move you took was wrong. We tend to have a misplaced perception that if we make a small investment, we equally receive small returns. Well, we have some trades that demand little from us and can result in huge incomes later on. We need to come to the point of understanding that the strategies that we utilize while trading can create

145

a huge impact on our trading career. With a small investment and the right strategies, one can make a huge impact as they would make with a huge investment. At times, it all narrows down to the mentality that we have and uphold regarding different instances in life.

Ignoring the Expiry Date

Trades have a certain period where they are regarded as valid; after this period, the underlying stock becomes useless. You might have purchased some stocks and failed to be keen on the expiry date. Before you know it, you end up making a big loss after your stocks have been regarded as invalid. This is a sad way to lose the money that you have invested in your stock. To avoid being caught up in such, you need to watch the stock market carefully and make a move when it becomes favorable to you. This way, you avoid reaching the expiry date with nothing. To accomplish this, one way is keeping a record of your trades. If this is something that you keep referring to on a daily basis, it becomes difficult to overlook some of these things.

Lack of an Exit Plan

We are too fast in identifying the signals that lead us to engage in a certain trade, but we barely take time to identify when to exit a trade. This is a mistake that we end up regretting deeply. Mainly, if you engage in a trade, it is expected that you identify all the factors that can sabotage what you have built. At times, you find that one is in a position to earn a lot from a particular trade strategy. However, if they keep holding on to their position, they may encounter a loss. To avoid finding yourself in such situations, learn to note the signals that point out that you need to leave a given trade. Staying will make things worse, so exiting is the best solution at this point. At times, you might be betting on the possibility of making a huge profit or making a huge loss. In such times, you would rather exit the trade and earn a small profit than take the risk of staying. When you stay, you might not be sure if you will earn a huge profit or experience a huge loss.

All of the above are some of the key mistakes that majority of us make while trading. However, if you feel like you are already making some of these mistakes, there should be no cause for alarm. I will provide some guidelines on how you can avoid making these mistakes while engaging in day trading options. There are more mistakes that traders make that have not been highlighted. You can learn more about them from other platforms. After all, as a trader, learning is something that you have to embrace.

How to Avoid Mistakes While Trading

1. *Plan ahead*

   There are numerous reasons that we should have a plan. Having a plan is not only applicable while trading, but it is essential in all aspects of life. Most of the mistakes traders make while trading can be resolved with the help of a good plan. When you can plan ahead, it places you in a better position of succeeding in the activity that you are undertaking. For instance, we can use the example of a team that is preparing for the finals. Getting to the finals happens to be the climax point of any team. For them to get to that point, it means that they must be among the best players who took part in the competition. Assuming that the team involved plays American football. As the final game approaches, the team has to come up with a plan that helps them take home the trophy at the end of the game. The coach has to identify each persons' strengths and know the spot where he can place each. At the same time, he has to ensure that he comes up with strategies that can give the team an upper hand over its counterparts. This is perhaps the most challenging thing that the coach will have to do. At the end of the day, the team with the best plan is likely to emerge the winner. You can travel to a given distance without a plan, but with a good plan, you can cover twice that distance.

On the other hand, a good plan helps in decision making. As a trader, there are a lot of decisions that you make, and they affect the outcome of what you are doing. The whole process of buying and selling stocks demands that you make wise decisions to ensure that you carry out successful trades. With the help of a good plan, you have a high likelihood of making the right decision regarding the trades that you make. In your plan, you could be having a journal where you write down each trade move that you make. The information that you get from the journal can be useful in tracking down different trades and seeing how you performed in each. You can easily identify the progress made and come up with ways where you can improve your trades. At the same time, you can identify the strategies that worked in different trades and those that were not the perfect choice depending on the situation at hand. This information is very beneficial and will create an impact on your different trades. Having a trading plan is essential, even if you are an expert. Most people believe that only beginners need to have a trading plan. However, this is a wrong belief. Each person who is conducting trades needs to have a trading plan for a smooth trading experience and to ensure that you do not make many trading mistakes

2. *Avoid covering up for losses*

At times, in life, things fail to move as planned. When this happens, it places us in a situation of feeling depressed and frustrated over the failures that we have encountered. Normally, in such a situation, the best thing would be to identify the mistakes that you made and decide not to make them again. We need to come to an understanding that we do not need to feel completely broken by bad situations, but instead, we should put on the full armor of positivity and turn the situation around to a lesson. Well, life, as it is, has never and will never be a walk in the park. We will encounter both good and sad days. The roads will be bumpy and, at times, smooth, but in both situations, we still have to get to our final destination. This means that in spite of the ups and downs that you will encounter, you still have to pick up your broken pieces and make something good out of them. In a situation where you encounter a setback, you will be tasked with turning the situation around into something good instead of allowing it to drag you down. There are moments when you will feel that the whole situation is beyond you and that you cannot handle it. However, you will have to learn to make it part of your growth. How does this relate to day trading?

In day trading, not all days will be full of successful trades. There are some days when you will encounter some losses. For some, they are not strong enough to handle the losses that come their way. You find that once they occur, they stay in denial, and they are unable to accept the turnout of events. This is mainly an issue with most beginners. At that point, there are a lot of trading mistakes that you are likely to make. You barely know much about trading at that point. At times, you make some trading moves that can sabotage your whole investment and take you back where you started. This mainly occurs when you do not take your time to master the art fully before investing in it. The majority of individuals make this mistake while starting out. There are a lot of expectations together with the excitement of starting to trade. In the process, you find that you trade with very little information. In such a situation, it is highly expected that anything can happen, and in most instances, it ends up in a loss. You decide that you will keep engaging in more trades, so you can compensate for the previous losses. While that happens, you end up losing more than you lost before. After a series of an unsuccessful trade, the best thing to do would be evaluating the mistakes you made in the previous trades so that you do not make them again. After carrying out this analysis, you can go ahead and make another trade.

3. *Decide the amount of money you can afford to lose*
   Money management skill is a skill that each trader needs. As an investor, you would like to see your investment grow to the levels that you expect it to go. At times, you will be required to keep reinvesting to double your income. For most investors, they survive on diversifying by being part of several ventures. For you to acquire wealth and sustain it, it demands that you keep developing what you already have and improve it. For instance, if I had $50 and invested it in options trade, I get lucky and walk away with $100 after a successful trade. Afterward, I go ahead and decide to invest in something different, such as dividend stocks. From the dividend stocks, I get $90 from an investment of $40. In this case, I will be increasing my income by engaging in different income-generating activities. Most individuals have managed to become wealthy from utilizing this strategy. At times, it is not how much you have to invest that counts, but how well to invest. Since it is expected that at the beginning of your trading journey, you are likely to have high expectations,

you want to ensure that you do it well so that you can walk away with huge sums of money at the end of the day. Making wise trade decisions will open doors for you that you never imagined would open.

Another mistake most people are making is buying cheap stocks. Buying cheap stocks is not always bad, but it is a problem if you are only limited to buying cheap stocks. Some people have a certain belief that one is highly unlikely to make a loss from cheap stocks. This makes them only go for cheap stocks while trading. In the end, they experience a loss since they did not consider other factors surrounding the trade. Some people go ahead and comfort themselves by saying that it was a cheap stock after all and that they did not make such a big loss. At times, cheap is equally expensive. For instance, you might have bought 7 cheap stocks. Supposing each went for $100, and you made a loss in all, this means that you have lost $700. At the same time, you may discover that there was one stock going for $350, and it had the potential of earning you a profit to get $1000. In such a situation, the best thing that you could have done was to go for the expensive stock instead of the cheap ones. While investing, ensure that if a loss occurred, you would still survive with the remaining amount. To some extent, depending on the circumstances of the trade, trading can be a gamble. You don't want to spend all your money on something that you are not certain about, which prompts the need to learn more about the strategies and how to go about trading.

4. *Avoid having too many expectations*

Incidences of overtrading and trading to cover up for a loss all result from having too many expectations. At times, we are overwhelmed by the numerous fantasies that we have. You are probably thinking of how you will travel the whole world with the money you get from trading options. Then again, you have heard numerous stories where people have made a fortune from day trading, and you decide that it will be the same for you. Well, it is not wrong to have such beliefs; the only thing that you need to do is ensure that you regulate the way you act based on these expectations. In some extreme cases, some individuals have acquired loans to get finances that they can use to trade. They know in their minds that after conducting a trade, they will get their returns. One thing leads to another, and they end up making a loss in the trade that they made. When this happens, the individual becomes frustrated, and at the same time, they do not know how they will repay the loan that they got from the lenders for trading. Such occurrences can place one in a difficult situation where they are unsure of the steps that they should take. If the individual had taken a different approach, this could have been avoidable. They would be in a better position in making sound decisions.

In this book, I have talked about the importance of classifying your dreams. In this case, you place your big dreams in the long-term category and those practical dreams in the short-term. By doing so, you can easily minimize your expectations. One day, you will get where you have always dreamed of. The only thing that you will do differently is trying not to break your back to attain what you want. You can hardly learn much from an instant success. While failure is not a good thing that can happen to anyone, we should learn to pick some lessons from it. Achieving growth is the process, and you need to appreciate each step that you make along the way. It is from the losses that you get to learn more about trading. At the same time, avoid taking huge risks since it might end up contrary to what you expected. As you aim to get to higher places, it is good to feel happy and content about the beauty of humble beginnings. You can easily start small as you grow and achieve more out of life. As you embark on a trading journey, you must be willing to push with the different ups and downs that you are likely to experience. At times, you may not get where you want fast enough; it will require that you learn to be patient. With time, as you keep learning and getting better, you will get to the levels that you aim.

Chapter 14: Leading a Successful Life

Success can, at times, be relative, depending on an individual's perception of what success is to them. As human beings, we are diverse in terms of our character, wants, needs, and goals in life. My idea of success may not be your idea of success. One fascinating thing about being human is that we have the power to choose how we define our journey here on earth. There are people who are living their best life, and at the same time, there are those who have totally missed the mark and ended up regretting the paths that they took. This brings us to the question: what brings the difference in the varying levels of achievement among people? There are many people who are craving for success, and I'm certain that you are among them. How do you get to achieve success based on your idea of it? Leading a successful life is not complex; it only requires that you know what you want in life, and you go for it. It is also important to note that nothing big was created by an individual that is not willing to make an effort. After identifying what you want, there is some effort that you need to put in place for you to ensure that you get to your desired level. Below are some factors that will help you lead a successful life.

5. *Know what you want*

Having an idea of what we want in life makes us understand what we are working for. A motivational speaker once visited a high school, and after his talk, he asked who needed a copy of his book. The majority of the students raised their hands, but one of them stepped forward to get the book. The speaker handed the book to the student and proceeded to say, "the only person who really needed the book is the one who came for it." From this story, we can establish that the first step into getting what we want is to know what it is and go forward to get it. There are different ways where we can establish what we want out of life. At times, it narrows down to the passion that we hold toward different things or the inclinations we have developed as we keep growing. In case you have difficulties finding out what you want, there are simple exercises that you can execute to help you identify what you are passionate for. For instance, you can hold a self-evaluation test. The test will require that you ask yourself some questions that can guide you to discover what you want. Some of these tests are available online. Basically, this should not be a tedious process that consumes much of your energy. By the time you are done with the test, you will have an idea of what you want to do.

Once you have identified what you want, the next step will involve putting it down on paper. I tend to believe that there is power in writing our dream and goals. For instance, you can make it your daily routine to go through the things that you would like to achieve. Such habits act as a daily reminder of what you are supposed to do and help you remain focused on achieving them at the end. There are times when we feel completely demotivated. For some, it's a daily struggle to wake up each morning because they are not motivated by the jobs, careers, or courses that they have chosen. You find it difficult undertaking different activities that do not inspire you in any way. We have had some people try to break free from such and decided to start a fresh page. Making such a decision is one of the most difficult things that one can do. You find that at that point, there is a lot of uncertainty, and you are not sure if you will regret the decision for the rest of your life. At the same time, there is a fear of failure. However, I am convinced that as long as one is passionate about what they do, they will achieve what they have set their eyes on. It's all about finding something that makes you feel motivated and going for it with courage and determination.

As you start your trading journey, you need to identify ways in which you can invest the money you get from trading. In most cases, we have people misusing the funds since it is quick money, and you probably think that you will trade again the next day and recover your money. Such perceptions have resulted in individuals remaining at a point of stagnation. This is where you live a hand-in-mouth kind of life. You earn a lot today and end up spending all of it at once, and the next day, you are at the same point when you began this journey. It is about time that we break from such destructive habits. Once you start investing in options trading, it is advisable that you know what you want out of that investment. This knowledge helps in proper planning and doing what is beneficial in one's life. With proper understanding and planning, you can make wise decisions with the money you get from investing. This helps you work more and increases your earnings, which, in turn, makes it a worthy investment.

6. *Be willing to learn*

Learning is one continuous process that never ends. There is no single person on earth who can confidently stand before people and claim that they have learned all that they could. The more we grow and advance, the more people come up with new things. There is an improvement on what is currently present, and at the same time, new things are coming up. With such advancement, it's difficult to exhaust everything that we need to know. This also applies to the options industry. Each day, we have new things coming up, and we need to keep us for us to remain in the game. Most trading experts will assure you that learning never stops, and neither does it ever end. As human beings, we should learn to embrace growth. Ideally, it is difficult to get anywhere when you are at a point of stagnation. Such points are limiting, and nothing good comes from them. Growth does not need to be a complex thing that you get to achieve all at once. At times, it comes in small steps, with each step holding a vital lesson that needs to be learned. You may feel like you are not getting it, but this is when you need to trust the process. It might be slow but sure, which means that at the end of it all, you will get the results that you are expecting. It is crucial to learn to understand the importance of humble beginnings.

While embracing the process of learning new things, you have to understand that you need to unlearn some things that we already know. Not every piece of information that we take in is accurate. Some information might be wrong and misleading, and we need to erase such information from our minds. When it comes to utilizing some trading strategies, you will learn that not all strategies will work in given instances. At the same time, a strategy that worked in a previous trade may not work in another trade. With such changes, one needs to keep up with the changing strategies and be willing to learn more strategies that they can utilize while trading. Having better knowledge about the industry gives you added advantage and places you at a better chance of succeeding in the trade. Most of the individuals who fail in trading never take the chance to learn more. They end up trading with little information and end up regretting after they encounter a loss. These are the same people that spread wrong information, claiming that trading is a scam, yet they never took their time to master the art before engaging in it. To avoid getting yourself in such a situation, be willing to learn. At the same time, ensure that you are consistent since new information keeps coming up with each passing day. This information should be applied to all aspects of life. For one to lead a successful life, they have to embrace learning new things each day.

7. *Stay positive and focused*

When was the last time you gave yourself a simple compliment? Well, I have realized that we are more invested in listening to what other people have to say about us, and we barely listen to ourselves. A simple "I can do this" reminder each morning can completely transform your life. It keeps you focused on what you do and makes you believe in your capabilities. Self-doubt had seen many people give up on their dreams long enough before they gave their first attempt. It has been proven to be an attribute that can result in self-sabotage at a very fast rate. We are at a point where staying positive seems like a difficult task to attain since we are all clouded with negative thoughts resulting from fear, uncertainty, and self-doubt. Many times, we tend to overlook it a lot, yet many are failing to chase their dreams because of these reasons. For instance, we know some individuals who are afraid of doing certain things just because other people tried and failed terribly at it. Recently, I came across an individual who was skeptical about engaging in options trading because he was afraid of failing like his cousin. I believe that another man's fate does not have to be your own. Just because another person failed at it does not mean that you will fail, too. We have to come to the point of defining our own paths. By doing so, we have to chase what we believe in without being held back by another person's failure.

You have probably heard of numerous speakers encourage people to stay focused. Why should we remain focused on the things that we do? There is a certain power that we generate from remaining focused. It allows us to stay rooted in our goals and ambitions. Regardless of what comes up, we are always motivated to learn more and do more. At times, we encounter various challenges that make us feel like quitting. For instance, you might have encountered a series of losses while trading and probably feel like giving up. However, with a positive attitude and a focused mind, you can easily pick yourself up and start trading again. Challenges are part of life. It is not every day that you will feel motivated or inspired. At times, you will be wondering why you got in some things in the first place. You will experience a lot of self-doubt along the way. However, you need to constantly remind yourself why you got in that journey. It is important to write down your goals at the start of anything. Whenever you go through them, they remind you why you started and help you to remain focused. Having a positive attitude makes the process easier since you always hope for a chance to do your best and you constantly believe that this will turn out as you expected. There is no easy journey, but it is that attitude and mentality that we hold that takes us where we need to be.

8. *Appreciate small wins*

Life can be moving on a fast lane, and we forget to take some time for ourselves. Most of us barely give ourselves enough credit after accomplishing something. At times, it is important to give yourself a pat on your back after accomplishing something. You find that we have big dreams, and we have this belief that the only time we can applaud ourselves is after accomplishing all the big dreams that we have. We fail to understand that success comes in steps. At times, the steps might be gradual, which means that we take more time to get to our desired destination. We have different goals and strategies; we may not all get to our idea of success as fast as we would want or expect. There are some challenges that we might encounter along the way, and hence, they slow us down. Some fantasies becoming an overnight millionaire may remain to be fantasies and never a reality. We need to be open to the idea that we may not always get what we want, and at times, even if we want it, it may not come as fast as we would expect. Slow but steady steps will eventually get us to our desired positions in life. This understanding allows us to appreciate growth. There is a lot that we can learn while embracing growth, and it can help us even when we become successful.

One other challenging situation that has caused many not to achieve their dream is the belief that they are in competition with others. Interestingly, we are all unique and different in our own ways. We do not think and behave in the same way, and neither do we uphold similar characters. Our life, on the other hand, never comes with a manual as to how we are supposed to live. We get in this world, and we are given the full responsibility of deciding who we become and what we want to be. Clearly, no one is told that they have to compete with anyone or ensure that they compare their life with another to gauge if they are accomplishing their goals. Comparison has killed many dreams here on earth. You badly want to be like someone else, and you forget that you have your own path to follow. I think it is about time that we learn to appreciate ourselves and believe in who we are. When you learn to have self-belief, you will be surprised by how much you can achieve on your own. You may not be the richest person in the world, but the basic act of appreciating the little that you have will help you learn how to get more.

Make it a habit of celebrating small achievements and see the impact it will have on your life. At the same time, learn what you can improve for you to keep winning at what you have committed yourself to do.

9. *Take responsibility for your actions*

At times, we tend to blame other people or things for the failures that we encounter in life. For instance, you make a loss while trading, and you start blaming things or people for the loss that you made. It is very easy to tie our failure on things, and we forget that we may also have a share in those failures. Holding a blame game will never give you the success that you thought you could have, but now, it is not. Perhaps, we should save ourselves from such thoughts and start taking full responsibility for our actions. Failure can be contributed by a variety of factors, and we do not have to tie it to only one. Such perceptions hold us back and prevent us from getting to places that we should be in, but we are not in them since we are always looking for a reason to pin our failure.

Failure is, at times, part of the success process. We are broken along the way before we get to our final destinations. Instead of feeling bad about failure, we should turn it into a learning opportunity where we get to learn from it and come up with ways to overcome it. Most traders encounter failure and decide to quit immediately. We fail to remember that it is a process and that before we become experts, we should brace ourselves for the challenges that we are likely to expect.

As we embrace failure and allow it to teach us instead of sabotaging us, we get to discover a lot. While trading, you can learn the strategies that worked and avoid those that did not work. You might also establish some patterns while trading that can guide you in learning the best time to trade. When you convert your failures into learning opportunities, there is a lot that you can pick from them that can lead you to successful trades. Since one can encounter some losses along the way, it is important to come up with ways where you can handle such incidences. For some, they end up in denial which later results in anxiety, depression, and trauma. Tying all your dreams and hopes in one thing can be damaging, especially if it fails. One needs to be open to more options and identify that if things fail to go as planned, there is still hope to redeem one's self. Many people fail to understand this, and hence, when they fail, they tend to think that it is the end of life. In case you are a victim of such beliefs, it is about time that you learn to break free from them before they become destructive.

We can all lead a successful life while doing the things we love, as long as we stay focused and disciplined in achieving our goals.

Conclusion

In case you have been struggling to understand how you can make it in day trading options, I hope you can now trade with confidence. The most important step in making a difference is having the willingness to learn. There is tremendous power in having information; it gives you an upper advantage in getting to places that you aspire to be in. With a determined spirit and mind, there is nothing that you cannot conquer. In this book, I have tried to give insight on different topics that relate to day trading. The majority of the information shared has been simplified in a way that is easy to understand. My aim is to create an impact on your life by transforming the way you trade. When you start to successfully make a living out of day trading, I would be delighted to know that I made a contribution to it. Like any investment, day trading has its own challenges. It is not every day that you will be smiling to the bank; you may encounter some gloomy days where things do not move as planned. At this point, you should be willing to learn and find out what it is that you are doing wrong. In the book, I have tried to explain the different strategies that you can utilize. The book also explained how day trading works in case there is anyone having difficulties mastering the art of day trading. You may not be an expert now, but with focus and a positive attitude, you will dine with the kings.

If you are looking for a quick way to make money, I will disappoint you by saying that this is not the venture that will get you that. One may argue that there are some people that have made a fortune very quickly. Well, I do not object; it is a good thing that they got lucky. However, as a newbie, having high expectations of quick results may cause you to be frustrated, especially if you do not achieve those results as fast as you had expected. For some, it takes time before they master the art and start making a fortune from trading. In case you got lucky and achieved a lot within a short duration of time, do not sell the idea that everyone can also achieve that as fast as you did. For some, it is a process, and they need to understand that it cannot work for them just because they did not get it as fast as you did. Trading is a skill that is learned by people who are focused and consistent at what they do. As a trader, whether an amateur or an expert, we all have to embrace learning. Gaining knowledge helps us achieve more and gets us to sharpen our skills. I hope that this book will make a difference in your trading life and that the information will lead you to successful trading.

Brandon Scott

Made in the USA
Middletown, DE
23 October 2021

50851448R00099